WINNING LIKE
SOURAV

Abhirup Bhattacharya is a graduate in fashion technology from the National Institute of Fashion Technology (NIFT), Kolkata, and has earned his MBA in finance from Narsee Monjee Institute of Management Studies (NMIMS), Mumbai. Beginning his career in the apparel sector in Egypt, he also has a diversified experience ranging from IT Consulting, Payment System and Risk Advisory and a passion for reading business books, writing stories, watching movies and cricket. He is also the author of *Winning Like Virat: Think and Succeed Like Kohli* (2017).

Hailing from the City of Joy, Kolkata, he is presently based out of Mumbai. He can be reached on Twitter @abhirupbh.

WINNING LIKE SOURAV

THINK & SUCCEED LIKE GANGULY

ABHIRUP BHATTACHARYA

Published by
Rupa Publications India Pvt. Ltd 2018
7/16, Ansari Road, Daryaganj
New Delhi 110002

Sales centres:
Allahabad Bengaluru Chennai
Hyderabad Jaipur Kathmandu
Kolkata Mumbai

Copyright © Abhirup Bhattacharya 2018

The views and opinions expressed in this book are the author's own and the facts are as reported by him which have been verified to the extent possible, and the publishers are not in any way liable for the same.

All rights reserved.
No part of this publication may be reproduced, transmitted, or stored in a retrieval system, in any form or by any means, electronic, mechanical, photocopying, recording or otherwise, without the prior permission of the publisher.

ISBN: 978-93-5304-106-9

First impression 2018

10 9 8 7 6 5 4 3 2 1

Printed at Parksons Graphics Pvt.Ltd., Mumbai.

This book is sold subject to the condition that it shall not, by way of trade or otherwise, be lent, resold, hired out, or otherwise circulated, without the publisher's prior consent, in any form of binding or cover other than that in which it is published.

To my parents & to all cricket lovers

Contents

Prologue / ix

Making of Brand Sourav / 1

Lessons in Leadership / 19

Mental Strength / 40

Quick Learner / 59

Risk Taker / 83

Grooming Future Leaders / 100

Power of Aggression / 116

Extra Special Sourav / 136

Acknowledgements / 146

Prologue

Sourav is a great captain and we should be proud of such a leader.
—Kapil Dev*

Sourav's greatest strength is his mind. He is hardworking—not only in the nets but also mentally. He bounces back.
—Sachin Tendulkar**

On the offside, first there is God, then Ganguly.
—Rahul Dravid***

'Dada, Dada, Dada…'

For any cricketing fan who has been to the Eden Gardens in Kolkata and has watched a cricket match in the early 2000s, such cheers should be reminiscent with the game. The atmosphere of Eden Gardens used to be electrifying each time Sourav

---

*https://www.sportskeeda.com/cricket/sourav-ganguly-the-man-who-introduced-dadagiri-and-redefined-indian-cricket
**https://www.sportskeeda.com/cricket/sourav-ganguly-the-man-who-introduced-dadagiri-and-redefined-indian-cricket
***http://www.cricketcountry.com/articles/15-memorable-quotes-on-sourav-ganguly-by-cricket-legends-517270

Chandidas Ganguly walked into the field. Once, Sourav was asked by Ravi Shastri, former Indian captain, why was there no stand named after him in Eden Gardens. Sourav had quite candidly responded that the entire ground belongs to him. Such a magnanimous statement could have only come from none other than the 'Maharaja of Indian Cricket'. Few people remember that Sourav scored just a meagre 3 runs in his international debut in Australia in 1992. His journey beyond that is for the history books—emerging as one of the finest Indian players ever to have played the game along with over 18,000 international runs. Quite a remarkable feat!

Hailing from Sourav's city, Kolkata, I too looked at him as a hero during my school days, and I still do. There often used to be debates about whether Sourav's form is declining in local *addas* and tea outlets across the city. He enjoys a cult status among all Kolkatans and in many ways cricket and Sourav Ganguly are synonymous to each other. While there might have been opinions on both sides of the argument, it was quite clear in the end of it that Sourav was special for any and every Kolkatan. He is the hero of the city and not just Eden Gardens. Kolkata loves the Maharaja. India also loves him and he's truly an Indian hero.

My first memory of Sourav dates back to his 1996 debut Test match at Lord's where he became one of the few Indian players to have scored a century on debut. This was no mean achievement considering that Kolkata was primarily known as a Football city and had not produced many cricketers who had done well at the international level. The strokeplay that was on display in seaming English conditions was a model to behold. If one looks at the command with which Sourav mastered the conditions, it was clear that Sourav belonged in the Indian dressing room for years to come. However, as fate would have it, Sourav was meant to change the past and create a new history of Indian cricket which will remain a legacy for generations of cricket lovers to come.

I did have the good fortune of watching him bat live few years after his debut at the Eden Gardens against Pakistan. Hardly anyone would have believed that the person who was unceremoniously dropped after just one ODI in 1992, along with questions over his attitude, would one day go on to emerge as one of the finest cricket captains of the modern era. Perhaps, it was this incident that was the backbone on which Sourav's mercurial rise and career would be defined in years to come.

Sourav Ganguly, apart from being one of the best left-handed Indian batsman India has ever produced, is also arguably one of the best captains who built the concept of Team India. Sourav ushered in the era where talented players were given a fair number of opportunities to prove their mettle in the dressing room. It is said that the true test of leadership is in the face of adversity. As a leader, Sourav grew out of adversity and led the team from strength to strength. He built the team from scratch with the help of young, talented players such as Yuvraj Singh, Harbhajan Singh, Virender Sehwag, Zaheer Khan and Mohammad Kaif. His ascent to captaincy was in the midst of the match-fixing controversy and yet, in a couple of years, he had rebuilt the team into a formidable opposition. He successfully led it to 11 overseas Test wins which remains the highest by any Indian skipper till date and also to the finals of the 2003 World Cup which India lost to the daunting Australian side. Yet, such an astute skipper not only lost his captaincy but also his place in the team in the Greg Chappell's era of Indian cricket.

While many of us would have given up at such a juncture,

Sourav was yearning to get back his rightful place in the team. His effort and desire was quite visible when he scored valuable 51 runs in the first innings of his comeback game against South Africa in 2006. This innings was largely responsible for ensuring an Indian victory against the Proteas in Johannesburg. Sourav retired on his own terms in 2008, ending a career spanning more than a decade and becoming one of the few cricketers to have played 100 Test matches. After retirement, Sourav remains associated with the game as part of various committees and currently as president of the Cricket Association of Bengal (CAB). His love for the game is well visible in his long standing association with the game. He is also an investor in a team in the Indian Soccer League. Apart from this, Sourav continues to be one of the highest paying retired cricketers and endorses several brands.

What drives him? How does he keep himself ready and motivated for the next challenge? When Sourav was dropped from the team, he could have simply given up. However, he decided to put up a fight and within six months the selectors could no longer ignore him. He faced a similar fate in the IPL 2009 when the then coach John Buchanan's multi-captain formula created another controversy. With over 7,000 Test runs, 11,000 ODI runs and 15,000 First Class runs, few can claim to have achieved such feat in their career. There is little doubt that he is one of the finest cricketers to have played and led by example in the modern era. Yet, he was neither the best batsman nor the quickest fielder. However, if you assimilate all his qualities, he was a force to be reckoned with. The one thing that exemplifies him is his belief and desire to answer his critics with his performance. He belonged to the era of Indian cricket marked by the greats like Sachin Tendulkar, Rahul Dravid, V.V.S.

Laxman, Virender Sehwag and Anil Kumble, and it is no mean feat to lead such legends.

Sourav, as an individual, signifies several qualities which include his aggressiveness and leadership skills apart from speaking his mind without mincing words. He believed that as a captain, it was his firm duty to back the youngsters like Yuvraj and Harbhajan and was quite clear in taking a stand on such issues. It is quite similar to a manager who ensures that his reporters are given the best opportunities depending on their skill sets. In his last international series against Australia in Border Gavaskar Trophy 2008, he scored 102 valuable runs (his 16th Test century) in Mohali, implying that there was still lot of cricket left in him. The 'Bengal tiger' was retiring on his own terms from international cricket.

Normally, every successful professional and individual writes their own fate through their actions and performances. As individuals, we encounter similar challenges in our work life which has its own peaks and troughs. The leadership lessons that Sourav provides can help in guiding any aspiring professional. There are valuable lessons that we can draw from his life in building a successful personal and professional career for us. His conduct has been exemplary and has always led by example. There is hardly any doubt that all of us would naturally accept and learn a lot if we have a leader like him in our lives.

His leadership skills can be best rated in the words of former Australian skipper Steve Waugh. It is notable that it was under Sourav that Australia's unbeatable streak of 16 Test matches came to an end during the famous Eden Gardens Test match in 2001. In the India Today conclave in 2016, Steve Waugh, when asked about Sourav, said:

> Ganguly was the first captain that changed the perception of the way India played their cricket.*

The statement is significant as it perfectly sums up the inspirational leadership that created the framework on which Team India is built today. In fact, the names 'Team India' and 'Men in Blue' were coined during his tenure, very much reminiscent of the coming of age for Indian cricket. Sourav is arguably one of the best captains to have ever played the game who could not lift the World Cup.

This book is not a biography of Sourav Ganguly. However, it is about the management lessons and inspiration that one can draw from the life of an exemplary skipper like Sourav. It is meant to guide us on how we can emulate the same lessons in our lives and become successful in our personal and professional sphere. It is highly recommended that one should read these lessons in the given order, reflect on them and then move on to the next chapter. There are key learning tips at the end of each section which will help the reader understand the key lessons. The book is not meant for any particular age group.

Happy reading!

---

*https://www.indiatoday.in/sports/cricket/story/conclave-2016-steve-waugh-opens-up-on-rivalry-with-sourav-ganguly-313751-2016-03-17

Making of Brand Sourav

> *Your brand is what other people say about you when you're not in the room.*[*]
> —Jeff Bezos, Founder of Amazon.com

What is a brand? A brand is a means by which an object or entity becomes identifiable. It can be a design, sign or symbol which distinguishes one entity from another. In short, it helps to create a distinction between two products. Branding is successful when we are able to associate the desired characteristics with a product. For example, each time we see a cola can, we are quick to differentiate between a can of Pepsi and Coke due to certain characteristics associated with each of them. In today's world, Amazon.com is rated as the most valuable brand in the world with a brand equity of $150.8 billion as per the 2018 Brand Finance Global 500 report.[**]

---

[*]https://www.marketingentourage.com.au/blog/what-do-people-say-about-you-when-you-leave-the-room
[**]http://brandfinance.com/images/upload/bf_global2018_500_website_locked_final_spread_03042018.pdf

Individuals are not different from companies in terms of branding. There are some individuals who have a cult following in their country. For instance, every time we see an image of Diego Maradona or Michael Jackson, we immediately recall the values of excellence and perfection that these two individuals are attributed with. While both these personalities emerged as the very best in their respective fields, they were equally shrouded by controversies. Similarly, there are some companies like Capgemini as well which use their employees for branding their firm. Even in our professional life, we normally associate certain qualities with those whom we encounter daily. One can easily remember the 'Hari Sadu' advertisement (2006) by naukri.com which had attributed the characteristics of a boss as per an employee. It showed an employee spelling out his boss's name by associating each letter to a negative characteristic of his boss. Clearly, individual branding can carry a positive or negative image along with strong and weak characteristics.

Sports personalities too are attributed with certain qualities. Usain Bolt might come to mind when we think of speed. In case of leadership with respect to cricket, we come across several great skippers like Imran Khan, Sourav Ganguly and Steve Waugh among others. However, what probably makes Sourav different from the rest is his ability to get reactions on both sides of a coin—there will be die hard fans of Sourav and an equal number of those who will oppose him tooth and nail. Almost any individual, who is aware of cricket, will have an opinion on Sourav Ganguly. He definitely has a strong brand recall.

Sourav's SWOT Analysis

The origins of brand Sourav can be decoded more aptly if we

perform a SWOT analysis on him. SWOT refers to Strengths, Weaknesses, Opportunities and Threats and can be used for understanding the various aspects with respect to any entity.

Figure 1.1
SWOT Analysis of Sourav Ganguly

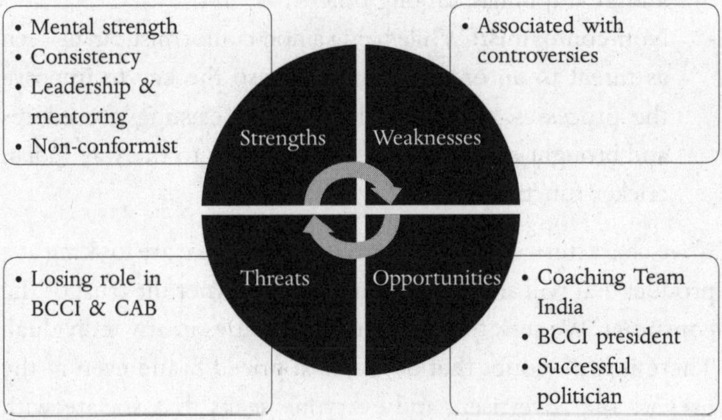

Strengths
- Mental strength
- Consistency
- Leadership & mentoring
- Non-conformist

Weaknesses
- Associated with controversies

Threats
- Losing role in BCCI & CAB

Opportunities
- Coaching Team India
- BCCI president
- Successful politician

Strengths

- **Mental strength:** It is said that more than 50 per cent of a sportsperson's success is attributed to how mentally strong he or she is in the team. The number of controversies and ups and downs that Sourav has handled in his career and bounced back each time, speaks volumes about his mental strength. Hardly any cricketer has undergone so much in his career—his perseverance speaks through.
- **Consistency:** Sourav has been an extremely consistent batsman averaging over 40 in both Test and ODI cricket, amassing over 18,000 runs in an international career spanning

over 13 years. When he has fallen short of runs while batting, he has compensated with his bowling techniques and has won matches.
- **Leadership and mentoring:** He has been one of the most successful captains in world cricket and has mentored the likes of proven match winners such as Virender Sehwag and Yuvraj Singh, among others.
- **Non-conformist:** While being a non-conformist can be seen as threat to an organization, it is also the key to improve the processes. Sourav challenged the existing procedures and brought about great deal of changes to the way Indian cricket functioned.

If we characterize these in terms of a brand, we are looking at a product that will always be desirable and garner the trust of the consumer. We seek these are prized qualities in any individual. There is little doubt that Sourav is a prized brand even in the eyes of the advertisers and everyone seeks to associate with him because of these qualities. If we look at automobile brand Porsche, it is able to retain its image and reliability by the use of high quality and unique materials, and provides its owners with not only a product, but an experience. To watch Sourav play the game and his conduct as an individual is similar to an experience few can afford to miss.

Learning Tip

There is nothing more important than performance and mental strength. Everything else is a result of the hard work that you put in when no one is watching.

Weaknesses

- **Associated with controversies:** Sourav's outspoken nature has often landed him in a number of controversies during his career and after retirement. While it may be part of his character to have no fear to voice his opinions, some of those controversies could have been avoided by curbing his outspoken nature. A few other controversies were fuelled due to vested interest of some people. For example, the 2017 controversy regarding the selection of the Indian coach and his support staff could have been avoided if not all parties (Sourav and others involved in the selection) had spoken to the press. Sourav's love-hate relationship with Greg Chappell too had begun with Sourav telling the media that he had been asked to step down. Sourav's illustrious career could have been longer if such controversies were avoided. However, it is equally a part of the 'Brand Sourav' that we visualize and find people having a love-hate relationship with the Bengal Tiger.

Learning Tip

You should know which battle to pick; if you end up fighting every battle, you will be wasting your time.

Opportunities

- **Coaching Team India:** His role as captain and mentor has impressed many and Sourav is certainly in the reckoning to coach Team India one day. He has also expressed on more than one occasion his desire to coach the team in future.

- **BCCI president:** Sourav is currently the president of the Cricket Association of Bengal (CAB) and he might go on to lead the BCCI one day. It would be a marked shift from the current scenario where politicians and industrialists are heading the governing body of the sport in India. As a former cricketer himself and being aware of the ground realities of facing young cricketers and the challenges ahead, Sourav would be able to highlight the issues that players experience and work towards the betterment of the game in general.
- **Politician:** Sourav has been offered a role in politics across the political spectrum. While he has so far declined it, he has campaigned in the past during elections. There was even news that Sourav had been offered the role of a sports minister by a certain political party if he contested and won in the general elections in 2014. Sourav has so far been reluctant in taking up a political career.

Threats

- **Losing role in CAB and BCCI:** Sourav has been quite outspoken so far about the role of administration and the changes that needs to be adopted. This might have created some rivals within BCCI. Moreover, the Supreme Court-appointed Committee of Administrators' decisions*, the Lodha Committee recommendations and issues such as conflict of interest (due to his various associations and advertising engagements) might impact his career as a cricket administrator.

---

*https://www.ibtimes.co.in/bjp-president-amit-shah-sourav-ganguly-bcci-top-brass-may-be-sacked-cricket-administrators-762584

Brand Attributes

If we look at the various roles that Sourav has played so far, we can further analyse the reason behind the strong brand equity for him.

- **Family man:** Sourav married his childhood sweetheart Dona and the marriage has lasted successfully ever since. His loyalty towards his love is unmatchable, coupled with his love and devotion to his daughter Sana. Whenever he finds time, he prefers spending it with his family. His personal upbringing in one of the richest families in Kolkata also contributes to his royal image.
  Brand attributes: Loyal, trustworthy and romantic
- **Cricketer:** Sourav led his team with distinction and delivered results. He guided and rebuilt Team India that was affected by the match-fixing controversy in the late nineties, led the team to the finals of Cricket World Cup 2003 and made successful comebacks when everyone had written him off. He has mentored some real cricketing talents, who have survived and made valuable contributions to Team India over these years.
  Brand attributes: Performer, leader, mentor and resilient
- **Administrator:** His short stint with CAB so far has been appreciated with several key achievements such as renovation of Eden Gardens and hosting the T20 World Cup. He is also a part of the BCCI cricket advisory committee and was instrumental in launching Vision 2020 to groom youngsters from West Bengal.
- As a co-owner of the football club ATK, Sourav was able to garner the combined support of East Bengal and Mohun Bagan fans for the new franchise. The feat is not a mean

achievement considering the fact that the two teams are always at loggerheads with a historical rivalry that dates back nearly 70 years.

When Sourav became chairman of the BCCI Technical Committee, he gave up on his commentating assignments as he did not feel it appropriate to continue with it. Sourav as commentator was extraordinary in his analysis and it was a treat for the audience to hear him. Clearly, he knows that his passion and love for the game is more than his personal interests.

In his tenure as the CAB president, Sourav has led the renovation efforts at Eden Gardens focussing on the comfort of spectators rather than the revenue. Post-renovation, the number of seats has reduced from 65,000 to around 37,000; while this may impact the revenue, it will certainly make watching the game more comfortable for the spectators. Clearly, Sourav is leaving no stones unturned in order to succeed in his new role.

Brand attributes: Strong manager, result oriented

- **Socially responsible:** Sourav has been vocal about his role as a responsible citizen of the country. His foundation (Sourav Ganguly Foundation) looks at providing free training to under-privileged children with a talent for sports. He has also been supporting campaigns such as 'Support My School', which focusses on improving the infrastructure of schools.[*]
  Brand attributes: Philanthropist
- **Investor:** Sourav has also invested in the Atletico de Kolkata (now called ATK, expanding to *'Amar Tomar Kolkata*: Yours and Mine Kolkata) team in the Indian Soccer League. He

---

*https://www.ndtv.com/supportmyschool/meet-the-ambassador

has recently invested in a Mumbai-based start-up Flickstree that works on video curation. In addition, he also runs his own restaurants in Kolkata under the name Sourav's.
Brand attributes: Entrepreneurial, risk taker

If we map his attributes in the form of a cloud, it will look like the following:

Figure 1.2
Attribute Cloud of Sourav Ganguly

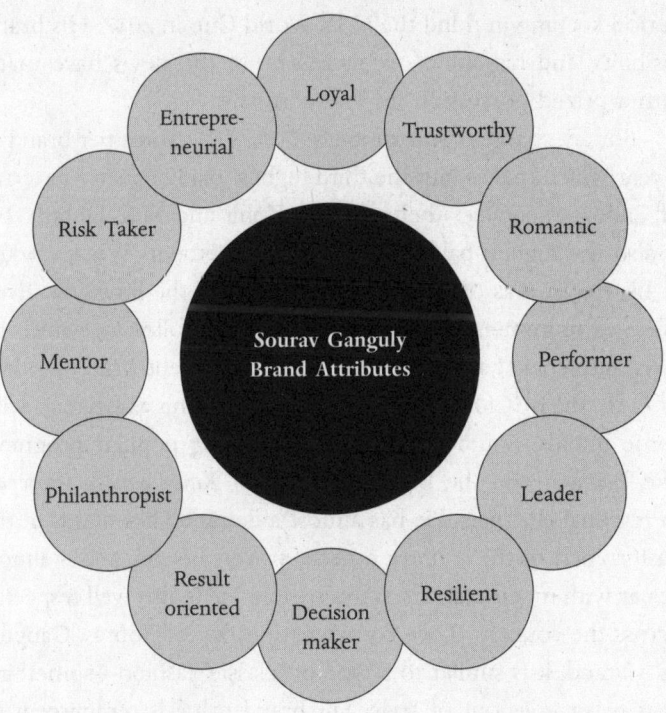

Brand Endorsements

Now, if we consider the brands that Sourav has endorsed so far in his career, it is evident that each of these brands signify some of the above-mentioned qualities. Sourav has been careful in selecting the brands that he has endorsed. Of course, none can forget the Hero Honda advertisement where Sourav shared the dance stage with actor Hrithik Roshan. Sourav's brand value also changed depending on the period of his career. Sourav was also made the social ambassador for Coca Cola for a 3-year period keeping in mind the U-17 World Cup in 2017. His brand visibility and his ability to always be in the news have made him a prized possession for any company.

Sourav charges approximately ₹1 to ₹1.5 crores per brand in a year which makes him the third-highest paid cricketer in terms of endorsement fees (behind Virat Kohli and M.S. Dhoni). He is also the highest-paid cricketer post-retirement. What worked in his favour was that he never went out of the limelight. Even after his retirement, he was part of the IPL following which he went into cricket administration. As he is currently the president of CAB, the BCCI has expressed concern over his association with some brands. Sourav has also been hosting popular programs like *Dadagiri* and the Bengali version of *Kaun Banega Crorepati* in regional channels. He has almost a demigod-like status in the eastern part of the country, especially West Bengal, and is almost at par with movie stars from this region. He is also well respected across the country. If we consider the story of Sourav Ganguly as a brand, it is similar to a type of 'classic' fashion—something that never goes out of style. His brand value is reminiscent of a timeless tale—it's like a legend whose tale grows with every passing day.

Figure 1.3
Brand Value Curve of Sourav Ganguly

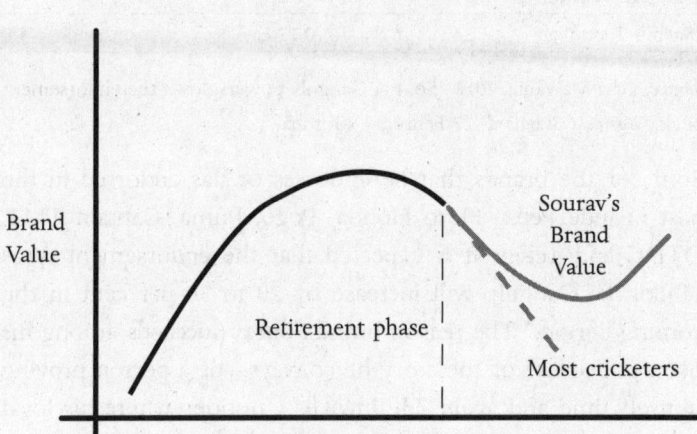

While for most cricketers, the brand value decreases exponentially after retirement, in Sourav's case, it has remained almost undiminished. This can be further substantiated if we consider the rate of endorsements* in comparison to other cricketers:

Table 1.1
Endorsement Fees of Various Cricketers

Cricketer	Endorsement Fee (₹)
Virat Kohli	10–12 cr
M.S. Dhoni	8–10 cr
Sourav Ganguly	1–1.5 cr
R. Ashwin	1.25–1.5 cr

*http://www.business-standard.com/article/specials/ganguly-powers-down-the-endorsement-pitch-117022600728_1.html

Suresh Raina	1–1.5 cr
Shikhar Dhawan	0.75–1 cr
Sachin Tendulkar	0.7–0.75 cr

Source: Urvi Malvania. 2017. 'Sourav Ganguly powers down the endorsement pitch.' *Business Standard*, 27 February. Mumbai.

Some of the brands that he endorses or has endorsed in the past include Pepsi, Hero Honda, Pogo, Puma, Captain TMT, DTDC and Tetley. It is expected that the endorsement rates of Sourav Ganguly will increase by 20 to 30 per cent in the coming period.* The reason brand Sourav succeeds among his peers is because of the story he conveys—of a person proving himself time and again. He invokes emotions where his loyal fans are willing to do anything to defend their beloved 'dada'. Most brands that associate with him aim to take advantage of the loyalty that he commands and hope that it would be reciprocated by the brands' followers. This story, however, would have been completely different if he had not made such a strong comeback to the Indian team. In fact, the story would have been that of any other cricketer, but Sourav's brand story was meant to stand out from the rest.

To tell a powerful story, brands need to be authentic. Nike and those alike, often use this technique where they try to tell a powerful story without mentioning their names until the last scene. Strong brands connect and resonate in the mind of the customer. Nike had even launched an equality campaign to celebrate the differences in the field of sports. In case of Sourav too, campaigns telling his stories have been done. Pepsico had launched a campaign with Sourav as the endorser which said,

---

*https://www.sportskeeda.com/cricket/sourav-ganguly-net-worth

'*Mujhe bhoole toh nahin*' (Hope you have not forgotten me). It was aimed at the people following the cola brand. The campaign had immediately struck a chord with the audience. It was telling the gripping story of a former captain who had been fighting hard to regain his place in the team. The message was clear and true; it further signified that Sourav had not given up. Even after his retirement, Apollo Munich Heath Insurance hospitals launched a campaign in a form of a movie on Sourav's life titled *Ganguly—The Movie*. The video has garnered over 1.5 million views and tells the gripping tale of Sourav with him sporting the brand's logo on his bat and t-shirt. People even commented on the video mentioning that they are looking forward to and are excited about the movie. He also has a documentary movie aptly titled *The Warrior Prince** based on his life and journey in cricket.

Learning Tip

To be a successful brand, you need to be authentic.

People love stories. In order to build any successful brand, customers need a story to connect with it. Even in corporate life, we look up to certain personalities because of their stories. It is the same reason why the Tesla founder Elon Musk is adored by millions all over the world. He tells the story of an entrepreneur building the future (by sending humans to another planet) and changing the way we look at it. If you have met or heard about the founder of your company, you would have often heard a story around it—how he or she has built the enterprise creating a value around the brand.

---

*http://www.imdb.com/title/tt5261646/ and https://www.youtube.com/watch?v=XBilETsSbPU

Social Media

Social media is an integral part of our lives in today's age. In less than 10 years, it has captivated and connected the world in ways that were unimaginable a few decades ago. Just like any brand understands the importance of social media, Sourav too has been quite active in connecting with his fans on social media.

His official accounts show the following statistics:

Facebook: 5,77,000+ likes*

Twitter: 3 million+ followers**

Sourav is not behind in ensuring his presence in social media in a strong manner and the numbers stand testimony to the fact. He regularly tweets and posts updates about his life on social media. This helps in keeping his fans updated about his activities thereby building a direct relation with the fans. He has also been using his social media presence to routinely showcase the work being done by his foundation and other philanthropic activities. Sourav has also launched his website souravganguly.co.in to further connect with his well-wishers. The corporate section of the website describes the cricketer in the following words: 'The name itself represents Trust, Passion, Courage, Reliability and Success'. He definitely understands his brand value and finds a way to connect with the corporate world for endorsements and the management as a speaker for leadership sessions.

Sourav understands personal branding beautifully and showcases his strengths perfectly. In today's world where everyone has a college degree, do they have a distinct personality?

---

*As on 13th May, 2018
**As on 13th May, 2018

It is here that personal branding comes into the picture. It can help any individual stand out from the rest. Social media networks provide a great means to build network and enhance personality with respect to your career. Thought leaders and industry stalwarts are now just a click away owing to platforms such as Facebook, Twitter, etc. Even though the question that remains is how to build a brand with a strong personality. Here are a few key steps:

- **Determine your expertise:** Make sure you understand your area of expertise. Every individual is blessed with at least one talent where he or she can outperform most. Social media provides an excellent platform to connect and learn from those who have succeeded in the same field. If you analyse Sourav's twitter profile, you will find him following a lot of sports personalities.
- **Be active:** Update your social media account regularly with posts related to your area of expertise. In addition, connect with those who are also posting on similar issues.
- **Maintain a strong offline presence:** Social media is there to complement your actual presence and increase your reach; it is not meant to substitute them. To build a strong brand, it is important to speak up at various professional events. This in turn helps in connecting with the target audience in a more effective manner and towards building authority on the subject.

Having a strong personal brand at the forefront of a sales campaign can have improved results. Steve Jobs used to utilize the same principle when he launched any product—his larger than life personality glued technology enthusiasts to their seats during the events. Similarly, Sourav's image will be in the forefront of any advertising campaign he is involved in. In the year 2014, Sourav also hired a management graduate from IIM Calcutta to build his own brand in his career as an entrepreneur.* Unlike most sportspersons, Sourav does not depend on external agencies but is keen to build it on his own.

Learning Tip
Use your social media presence wisely; invest time in it to build a brand for yourself.

Sourav's story tells us how to stay relevant in the market. It provides answer to few key questions which others can follow and try to emulate:

- **Your current brand identity:** What do you like about it? What is it that you hate about it? It is important to understand your current stakeholders and shape your brand's identity accordingly. In order to be successful, you need to keep reinventing yourself. You need to introspect and build an image for yourself in the company you are working.
- **Your story:** Your story should be authentic. Always be proud of your own story; your beginnings and your journey—the foundation on which your story is built on. All of us are unique in our own ways; there is no need to impersonate anyone else.
- **Your role model:** One needs to have an ideal whom

---
*https://www.firstpost.com/economy/sourav-ganguly-hires-iimc-graduates-for-his-brand-management-1961653.html

one can follow. If you seek to be a sports personality, you will be keen to model yourself on the lines of a former sportsperson. Likewise, if you seek to be an entrepreneur, a role model in the same field will inspire you. This will serve you as a guide in your mission. Sourav looked up to his father as his role model along with various legendary cricketers from his childhood days.
- **Your goal:** The goal or target should be clear and well-defined. This will ensure that your image is built accordingly and you take the right decisions.

Brand Sourav—Future and Beyond

Sourav's brand story is similar to a sinusoidal curve which oscillates with every change in his fortune. We too need to look at every turn our careers take and make decisions that will help achieve objectives. Sourav's goal was to play for the country; he achieved it. Other events such as captaincy came as a result of his performance. Every brand is built around the objective it intends to achieve. To build a successful brand at workplace, one needs to work and timely deliver results.

Sourav's career consists of three distinct phases:

- The first international stint in Australia in 1992
- Subsequent dream-run in Indian cricket
- Fairy tale return and post-retirement

Figure 1.4
Sourav's Brand Value Swings in Different Phases

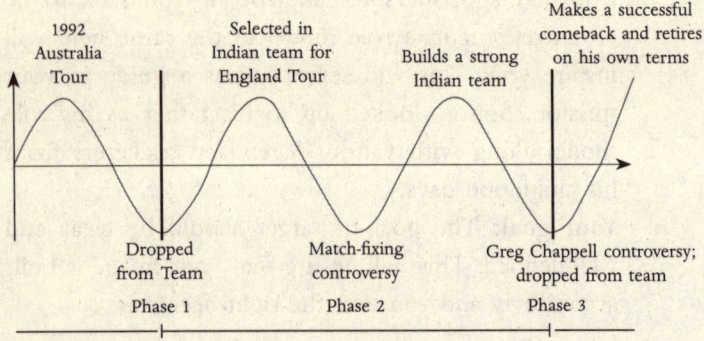

The tale of the first-two phases is mostly same in anyone's life, but it is the last phase that makes the difference. It is what the brand story is all about—someone who never gives up in the face of adversity and is willing to give back more than he has received. That's what the brand Sourav is all about. If you feel you understand the brand today, think again for he may spring up another surprise. After all, he is 'the warrior prince'.

Lessons in Leadership

A leader is one who knows the way, goes the way, and shows the way.

—John C. Maxwell, American author and speaker

Leadership is the art of motivating others and driving them towards achieving their true potential. It refers to the ability of an individual to guide others. A sport is a team game and building a successful team is just like running a business. In order to deliver results, it is important to have different departments working together towards a common objective. The impact of leadership can best be observed if we consider the case of Chinese appliance-maker Haier. The company was inching towards bankruptcy when Zhang Ruimin took over as the General Manager of the troubled company. In order to drive the point that poor quality will not be tolerated, he got his workers to destroy 76 defective refrigerators with sledgehammers. He wanted the workers to feel what it is like to destroy something they have themselves built. He wanted them to understand the value of quality. It was this decision that led

Haier to emerge as the world's largest manufacturer of white goods three decades later. He had not reinvented anything, but he provided the workers direction which helped the company to grow. His philosophy was simple 'Challenge yourself, overcome yourself'. Leaders such as Zhang are rare. They have the gift of inspiring others to achieve more than they aspire or hope for.

Can leadership be taught or is it a quality that people are born with? Leadership in any individual is shaped based on two things—the surroundings we are brought up in and its impact on us. For example, if we consider the leadership of Ratan Tata of Tata Group, we inevitably find him a calmer individual as compared to Elon Musk or Richard Branson. All three of them are exceptional leaders to the core but have phenomenally different styles of dealing with a situation.

Individual sports such as tennis or badminton are more of a game of power and skill rather than leadership. In sports such as these and by virtue of their nature, the sportsperson is more concerned about his or her performance rather than that of others. Football and cricket, on the other hand, are entirely team games and without a strong leader and captain, the team will falter no matter how skilled the individual players are. In order to get the desired outcome, it requires a great tandem with a variety of skills and playing techniques among individuals of different backgrounds. In fact, a golden rule of putting together a side in a team sport is based on choosing individuals who prefer 'we' over 'me'. There have been several great captains in world cricket like Sir Donald Bradman, Clive Lloyd, Imran Khan, Alan Border, Arjuna Ranatunga, Steve Waugh, Sourav Ganguly, Ricky Ponting, Stephen Fleming and Mahendra Singh Dhoni. Few of them had built a side from a scratch. Even fewer have led the side from a crisis to a new direction. Sourav Ganguly can lay claim to both the feats. Just like a watchful captain of a ship, he has guided his ship to safe anchor and built the foundations of Team India as we know it today.

The Game of Numbers

Numbers often tell a story. It is the only way to distinguish a fact from a fiction. Just like companies are driven by balance sheets and profit & loss statements, captains are rated based on their success rate. Sourav's captaincy record speaks for itself. If we consider Test cricket and compare his record with all Indian captains over the years, Sourav emerges as the third most successful captain in terms of win percentage and the second most successful captain in terms of win/loss ratio. Sourav's win/loss ratio is even higher than that of M.S. Dhoni and still holds the record of highest number of wins overseas as a Test captain. Virat Kohli though is expected to break the latter record in coming years.

Table 2.1
Success Rate of Various Indian Captains in Test Cricket as of 10 February 2018 (in terms of the most recent captain)

Player	Period	Mat	Won	Lost	Tied	Draw	W/L	%W
V. Kohli	2014–18	35	21	5	0	9	4.2	60
M.S. Dhoni	2008–14	60	27	18	0	15	1.5	45
S.C. Ganguly	2000–05	49	21	13	0	15	1.61	42.85
R. Dravid	2003–07	25	8	6	0	11	1.33	32
M. Azharuddin	1990–99	47	14	14	0	19	1	29.78
B.S. Bedi	1976–78	22	6	11	0	5	0.54	27.27
A.L. Wadekar	1971–74	16	4	4	0	8	1	25

Nawab of Pataudi	1962–75	40	9	19	0	12	0.47	22.5
A. Kumble	2007–08	14	3	5	0	6	0.6	21.42
D.B. Vengsarkar	1987–89	10	2	5	0	3	0.4	20
S.M. Gavaskar	1976–85	47	9	8	0	30	1.12	19.14
N.J. Contractor	1960–62	12	2	2	0	8	1	16.66
S.R. Tendulkar	1996–2000	25	4	9	0	12	0.44	16
L. Amarnath	1947–52	15	2	6	0	7	0.33	13.33
N. Kapil Dev	1983–87	34	4	7	1	22	0.57	11.76
V.S. Hazare	1951–53	14	1	5	0	8	0.2	7.14

Key: Mat=Matches, Won=Matches won, Lost=Matches lost, Tied=Matches tied, Draw=Matches drawn, W/L=Matches Won/Matches Lost, %W=Win percentage

If we consider his ODI record as captain, it is no less impressive. Sourav comes across as the third most successful captain in terms of the number of matches won.

Table 2.2
Success Rate of Various Indian Captains in ODI Cricket as of 10 February 2018 (in terms of the most recent captain)

Player	Period	Mat	Won	Lost	Tied	NR	Win/Loss	% Win
V. Kohli	2013–18	47	36	10	0	1	3.60	78.26
M.S. Dhoni	2007–16	199	110	74	4	11	1.49	59.57
R. Dravid	2000–07	79	42	33	0	4	1.27	56
N. Kapil Dev	1982–87	74	39	33	0	2	1.18	54.16
M. Azharuddin	1990–99	174	90	76	2	6	1.18	54.16

S.C. Ganguly	1999–2005	146	76	65	0	5	1.17	53.9
S.M. Gavaskar	1980–85	37	14	21	0	2	0.67	40
S.R. Tendulkar	1996–2000	73	23	43	1	6	0.53	35.07

Key: Mat=Matches, Won=Matches won, Lost=Matches lost, Tied=Matches tied, Draw=Matches drawn, W/L=Matches Won/Matches Lost, %W=Win percentage

In terms of contemporary Indian cricket post-2005, both M.S. Dhoni and Virat Kohli have been extremely successful in comparison to their predecessors in both Test and One-Day cricket. However, while Dhoni and Kohli inherited a strong Indian team as captains, whereas Sourav did not have such a luxury. Some of the players who used to form the core of the Indian team were mired in the match-fixing controversy. Sourav persisted with youngsters to fill in those slots as a result of which his winning percentage was low in the initial years. Later, these cricketers played a significant role in ensuring the winning streak under M.S. Dhoni's captaincy. Sourav's team was very similar to a start-up which was building a product and looking for core members; Dhoni's team was similar to such a setup receiving funding from investors; and under Kohli, it is finally delivering returns for the investors. In any organization, while a team is being built, the management remains patient for initial years and believes in positive outcome in the later years. Same is true in a sport like cricket.

If we compare Sourav's record with his counterparts globally, he has one of the finest records. For the purpose of comparison, only those captains who have led the team in 100 or more ODI matches, or 40 or more Test matches have been considered. In terms of win percentage, his record may look average, but considering the fact that he led a young side and still managed a win percentage exceeding 50 is commendable.

The more apt comparison will be if we look at the records of Imran Khan, Arjuna Ranatunga and Stephen Fleming along with Sourav since each of them inherited a very young team and built it into a world-beating squad. They were all reminiscent of time-tested CEOs. Sourav has the highest winning percentage among these skippers which speaks volumes of his leadership considering Test matches are the true test of their capabilities. At the same time, it will be unfair to rate any of these skippers better than others as all of them were equally capable of leading the side under difficult situations and delivering results.

Table 2.3
Success Rate of Sourav with Contemporary Captains in Test Cricket

Player	Span	Mat	Won	Lost	Tied	Draw	W/L	%W	%L
S.C. Ganguly (IND)	2000–05	49	21	13	0	15	1.61	42.85	26.53
SP Fleming (NZ)	1997–2006	80	28	27	0	25	1.03	35	33.75
Imran Khan (PAK)	1982–92	48	14	8	0	26	1.75	29.16	16.66
A Ranatunga (SL)	1989–99	56	12	19	0	25	0.63	21.42	33.92

Key: Mat=Matches, Won=Matches won, Lost=Matches lost, Tied=Matches tied, Draw=Matches drawn, W/L=Matches won/Matches lost, NR=No Result, %W=Win percentage, %L=Loss percentage

The one area that Sourav however lacked was his performance as a player who suffered during captaincy. There is a stark difference in his performance as a player and a captain over the years. From 2000 to 2005, his average varied significantly and reached a mere 24.9 in 2005—the same year when Sourav was dropped from the team.

Table 2.4
Sourav's Performance in Test Cricket over the Years

Year	Mat	Inns	NO	100s	50s	0s	HS	Runs	Avg
1996	6	11	1	2	1	2	136	504	50.4
1997	11	15	0	3	3	1	173	848	56.53
1998	5	9	1	0	1	0	65	267	33.38
1999	10	19	3	2	7	1	125	813	50.81
2000	6	10	1	0	2	0	84	279	31
2001	13	23	3	0	1	2	98*	444	22.2
2002	16	25	2	2	5	2	136	945	41.09
2003	4	7	1	2	1	0	144	393	65.5
2004	8	9	0	0	4	0	88	408	45.33
2005	7	10	0	1	0	0	101	249	24.9
2006	4	6	1	0	1	1	51*	173	34.6
2007	10	19	1	3	4	0	239	1106	61.44
2008	13	25	3	1	5	4	102	783	35.59
13 Years	113	188	17	16	35	13	239	7212	42.18

Key: Mat=Matches, Inns=Innings, NO=Not outs, 100s=Hundreds, 50s=Fifties, HS=Highest Score, Runs=Runs scored, Avg=Average

His ODI performance over the years also looks similar to his Test record.

Table 2.5
Sourav's Performance in ODIs over the Years

Year	Mat	Inns	NO	100s	50s	HS	Runs	Avg	S/R
1992	1	1	0	0	0	3	3	3	23.08
1996	10	9	1	0	2	59	269	33.63	62.56
1997	38	35	3	1	10	113	1338	41.81	69.72
1998	36	35	3	4	7	124	1328	41.5	69.78
1999	41	41	3	4	10	183	1767	46.5	76
2000	32	32	4	7	6	144	1579	56.39	82.76
2001	23	22	0	2	6	127	813	36.95	71.07
2002	32	30	1	1	9	117*	1114	38.41	82.7
2003	22	22	4	3	2	112*	756	42	76.21
2004	31	30	1	0	7	90	947	32.66	69.89
2005	13	13	1	0	1	51	209	17.42	54.71
2007	32	30	2	0	12	98	1240	44.29	73.03
12 Years	311	300	23	22	72	183	11363	41.02	73.71

Key: Mat=Matches, Inns=Innings, NO=Not outs, 100s=Hundreds, 50s=Fifties, HS=Highest Score, Runs=Runs scored, Avg=Average, S/R=Strike Rate

Was captaincy affecting his performance? Was Sourav unable to bear the burden of leading the side much like Sachin before him? There are a couple of reasons for the decline in his average. Sourav sacrificed his batting slots in both Test and ODI line-up in the interest of the team. This, as a result, impacted his performance. He was of the view that the focus should be on building a formidable team rather than on his performance. After all, had performance been the only criteria for playing in the team, why had he been dropped in 2007, in spite of having over 1,000 runs in ODI and Test cricket? In business as well, it is sometimes important to market yourself to the management for the quality of work you have been demonstrating. For example, issues are bound to arise while tackling client expectations in a difficult project. In such a scenario, as a project leader, your ability to resolve such issues becomes critical. It is equally important for the management to know the efforts that have been put in to achieve the desired outcome. This helps in maintaining your visibility in the organization and the value you bring into the team. It is very easy for an outsider to criticize the efforts made by someone without knowing the challenges in delivering the project.

Learning Tip
It is important to market your qualities and work in your organization to ensure you receive proper visibility.

Many have criticized his ability to handle pressure along with captaincy, but the numbers tell an entirely different story. If we look at his performance against all the major cricketing nations in ODIs, his average is consistent (except Australia) with 22 centuries and 72 half-centuries. While it is true that he could have scored more runs in Test cricket, he has missed deserving centuries by a very small margin in many occasions.

Table 2.6
Sourav's Performance in ODI against Various Teams

Versus	Mat	Inns	NO	100s	50s	0s	HS	Runs	Avg	S/R
Australia	35	33	0	1	5	3	100	774	23.45	67.72
Bangladesh	10	10	2	1	4	1	135*	459	57.38	75.62
England	26	26	1	1	7	1	117*	975	39	76.11
New Zealand	32	31	1	3	6	3	153*	1079	35.97	74.21

Versus	Mat	Inns	NO	100s	50s	0s	HS	Runs	Avg	S/R
Pakistan	53	50	3	2	9	4	141	1652	35.15	71.83
South Africa	29	29	3	3	8	1	141*	1313	50.5	76.56
Sri Lanka	44	40	2	4	9	3	183	1534	40.37	72.53
West Indies	27	27	3	0	11	0	98	1142	47.58	72.19
Zimbabwe	36	36	4	3	7	0	144	1367	42.72	74.82
Overall (17)	311	300	23	22	72	16	183	11363	41.02	73.71

Key: Mat=Matches, Inns=Innings, NO=Not outs, 100s=Hundreds, 50s=Fifties, HS=Highest Score, 0s=Ducks, Runs=Runs scored, Avg=Average, S/R=Strike Rate

Key for Sourav's Success

- **Being adaptable:** In order to look at a successful leadership model, we need to understand the influence of Generation X and Generation Y leaders in a team. Generation X leaders are hard task masters who believe that in order to deliver results, one must push and drive the team members. Imran Khan could be considered as such a leader who was autocratic in many ways. However, his style was focussed as a means for building the team and maintaining discipline in the mercurial side. Generation Y, on the other hand, believes that people are motivated by themselves. Google is a fine example of a company which promotes and encourages such a culture. It is one of the key reasons for its innovative products where people are encouraged to think out of the box.

    A leader like Sourav lies at the intersection of Generation X and Generation Y leaders. Belonging to a wealthy and prosperous family, the art of leading and commanding came to him naturally. There was always a royal flavour to his attitude which observers often misconstrued as arrogance. At the same time, he was open to hear others' perspectives as was evident in the dressing room discussions as well as on the field. He believed in his players and the players believed in his team. If we try to plot his leadership style using Venn diagrams, it will look something similar to this:

Figure 2.1
Sourav's Leadership vs Gen Y and Gen X Leaders

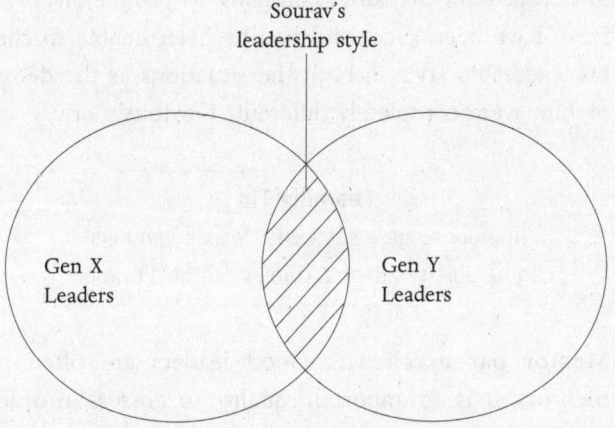

Leaders who are successful usually combine both aspects of Gen Y and Gen X to emerge as more successful. It is extremely important that leaders have the flexibility to adjust themselves according to a situation. In the Indian team that Sourav led, there were experienced players like Sachin Tendulkar and Anil Kumble as well as a youngster such as Mohd. Kaif. In a situation as such would he have been successful if he was always strict and not followed a consultative approach? Good leaders are always able to adjust and mould themselves according to the demands of the situation. When Steve Jobs co-founded Apple Computer Inc. he was building a start-up. Apple intended to disrupt the market with products which were far superior to those available. Steve was known for his presentation skills and exuberance which helped in building the company as a leading firm. However, after a subsequent fallout with the then CEO John Sculley, Steve had to leave the company in 1985. Years later, when he returned to Apple in 1997, he turned around the same company to profitability. Would Steve have been successful had he been unable to change his leadership style in both the situations as the demands of him were completely different? Obviously not!

Learning Tip

In order to be a successful leader, you need to be able to adapt according to the situation

---

- **Mentor par excellence:** Good leaders are often great mentors. It is an important quality to possess in order to build a great team. Imran Khan, for instance, mentored a young cricketer from Multan in the 1992 World Cup. The young lad wasn't sure if he was good enough for the level Imran wanted him to play at. Imran said that had he not been good enough, he wouldn't have been here. The young lad outperformed everyone in the semi-finals and ensured the victory for Pakistan in the 1992 World Cup. His name was Inzamam-ul-Haq—one of the greats of the modern game. Former Sri Lankan captain Arjuna Ranatunga also led an extremely young side to the World Cup glory in 1996. His experience along with a handful of seniors played an important role in shaping the youngsters in the team. If you want to progress in your career having a mentor is essential. We often find individuals doubting their capabilities in a new environment; if someone with experience guides them, it makes a world of difference in their lives. It helps them in finding a direction and ways to do things differently.

In the documentary *The Warrior Prince*, Virender Sehwag tells of an incident in Pakistan when Sourav asked him if he was facing any issues and that if he could help in any way. Former Indian wicketkeeper Syed Saba Karim too speaks on similar lines of the times when Sourav used give him tips standing on the first slip and suggestions based on the match situation. It was during Sourav's tenure that several youngsters came to the fore and created a new core for the team. He was able to create a blend between the seniors and juniors in the team. The team looked up to him for guidance in moments of crisis.

Sourav's mantra was simple: If he believed that a youngster was talented, he would have enough opportunities to prove his worth. This provided a much-needed calmer atmosphere for the young player as it was certain that he will not be dropped after one failure. M.S. Dhoni is a fine example of this policy. Despite failing in his first four innings, Sourav decided to pursue with the youngster who repaid with a 148-run knock against Pakistan. It was one innings which probably set Dhoni's career on a completely different trajectory. Dhoni went on to lead the country to two successful World Cup victories—ICC T20 World Cup and World Cup 2013. If Sourav had not persisted with him, India would have arguably lost its finest wicketkeeper-batsman till date.

It is equally important to have a mentor to succeed in corporate life. Current CEO of Pepsico Indra Nooyi credits the mentoring that she received throughout her corporate career for successfully breaking the glass ceiling.

Learning tip

In order to build a successful team, you need to mentor and lead the youngsters in it.

- **Building relations:** It is said that in order to travel fast, one should be alone. But if one has to journey far, it is extremely important to travel as a team. If you consider any leading organization, you will see that it is being driven by an enterprising leader, backed by an equally talented and enthusiastic team. In order to achieve any dream, one needs to find like-minded people who can share the vision. Consider for instance, the global e-commerce giants like Alibaba and Amazon with workforce across the global, comprising the best talent pool in the world. In such a scenario, differences in opinions and ego clashes are quite common. Former Apple co-founder and CEO Steve Jobs used to feel the same. In his words: 'It's not about money. It's about the people you have, and how you're led.'*

  In order to build and lead any team, a leader must inspire

---

*https://en.wikiquote.org/wiki/Steve_Jobs

team spirit. Would you prefer to work for a boss who is self-centred or one who believes in taking everyone along? The answer is fairly simple. Building relationships play a significant role in ensuring growth in any organization. Just like vendor or client relationship is important, having a healthy working relationship among team members is crucial for the success of the team.

If we ignore the controversy surrounding coach Greg Chappell, Sourav managed to create a healthy working relationship with coach John Wright in building the new team. It was the first time that Team India was having a foreigner as its coach; and the captain-coach duo together stitched the glorious years of Indian cricket. Sourav focussed a lot on building interpersonal relationships with his teammates and went on to create 'Team India'. The country started playing as a team under his leadership and was no longer solely dependent on the batting prowess of Sachin Tendulkar. On one hand, he was handling the match-fixing crisis by restoring public's faith in the team; on the other hand, he was building the foundations of a democratized team selection based purely on merit.

Learning tip

Focus on building interpersonal relationships at work.
It helps in delivering results and retaining the best people.

- **Sharp strategist:** Sourav had one of the sharpest–cricketing minds who could foresee the situation and make changes in his team accordingly. Some of his strategic decisions were as follows:

- In the 2001 Border-Gavaskar trophy series against Australia at home, he felt Harbhajan would be a significant force to ensure a favourable outcome, whereas for the 2003–04 series against the same team, he preferred Anil Kumble in overseas conditions.
- In order to create a more devastating opening combination, he was willing to sacrifice his slot to Virender Sehwag and move to No. 3 in ODI line-up. Later, he gave up the No. 3 slot in favour of M.S. Dhoni. Sourav always put the team first.
- He deliberately came late for the toss in the 2001 series against Australia to influence the Australian captain Steve Waugh. In a similar spirit, he was quick to respond to all verbal assaults and mental games by the Australian team in 2003–04 Border–Gavaskar series.
- Early on in his captaincy career, in order to ensure balance in batting order and give greater flexibility in the team, he opted for Rahul Dravid as wicketkeeper in the ODI team. This was also one of the reasons for India's progress until the finals of 2003 World Cup.
- He was willing to have a foreign coach in the form of John Wright and later Greg Chappell to ensure neutrality in the selection of the team and bring in new approaches. While the decision to go ahead with John provided rich dividends, the Chappell move backfired.

Strategy plays an important role in cricket. One can analyse as much as one wants from the dressing room but eventually the captain has to make the decisions. Amidst the fan frenzy, modern-day cricket captains are no less than generals leading armies to the battlefield. It was during Sourav's tenure that India emerged as a strong fielding squad with specialized positions at cover and point for the likes of Mohd. Kaif and Yuvraj Singh. Sourav marshalled his resources well under tough conditions which can be attributed to his higher success rate in Test matches overseas.

Table 2.7
Sourav's Test Captaincy Record (Overseas) with Other Indian Captains

Players	Matches	Won	Lost	Drawn	Loss%	Win%
Sourav Ganguly	28	11	10	7	35.70	39.30
Mohd. Azharuddin	27	1	10	16	37.04	3.70
M.S. Dhoni	30	6	15	9	50.00	20.00
Virat Kohli	16	8	4	4	25.00	50.00

In a similar manner, strategy plays an important role to ensure that any particular product does well in the market—right from its launch to distribution and finally to the marketing campaign. Consider for instance, the strategy behind the food retail giant McDonalds to launch products such as 'Aloo Tikki' only for the Indian market. It has helped the company to establish itself as a household brand in urban India with the product along with other local items accounting for more than 50 per cent of its annual sales.* The success of the product prompted the company to introduce the same in other markets like the Middle East. For an individual too, it is the choices that make them. The choices we make are nothing but the strategies we adopt for ourselves. If we are given the option of joining either Company A or Company B, the decision will be based

---

*https://retail.economictimes.indiatimes.com/news/food-entertainment/food-services/mcaloo-tikki-sandwich-becomes-part-of-mcdonalds-battle-with-local-partner-vikram-bakshi/24178182

on which firm will help us achieve our goals. In short, it will be our strategic decision.

Learning Tip

Whenever faced with a choice, consider all possible outcomes before making the relevant choice.

- **Sourav's leadership style:** In the book *Primal Leadership* by Daniel Goleman, Richard Boyatis and Annie Mckee, the authors talk about six different leadership styles. Four of these styles are resonant in nature (visionary, coaching, affiliative and democratic), whereas two of the styles are dissonant (pacesetting and commanding). If we consider the characteristics of Sourav, he combines each of these styles to perfection in order to emerge as an effective leader.

Figure 2.2
Sourav's Leadership Style

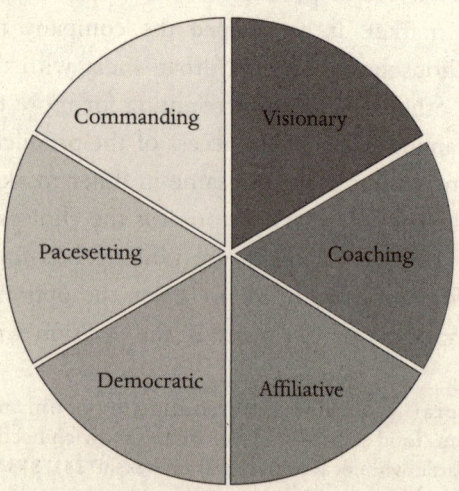

- Visionary: He created the vision of building a team that will be a formidable force both at home and overseas.
- Coaching: He believed in mentoring and guiding the youngsters.
- Affiliative: He believed in ensuring harmony in the team and in building relationships.
- Democratic: He ensured that youngsters could freely raise their opinion on any issue. This is extremely important for any team as the best idea can come from anyone.
- Pacesetting: He believed in leading from the front both as the captain and with his batting performances. His performance in high pressure matches against Pakistan stand testimony to this.
- Commanding: Sourav reserved his commanding style only with respect to team selection. When he was not playing cricket, he was extremely accessible and led a simple lifestyle.

In a similar manner, as individuals, we too need to sometimes combine one or more of these characteristics in our leadership style depending on the situation. In order to be a successful leader, one must have the following attributes:

- Good communication skills
- Vision for the team
- Trusted and respected
- Open and willing to hear
- Positive and optimistic
- Can accept responsibility and give credit
- Creates a team based on different qualities of individuals
- Does not impose authority

There is little doubt that Sourav Ganguly, with his exceptional leadership style, was instrumental in bringing about a transformation in the Indian team. He built the team that believed in winning matches overseas. Whenever the team won, Sourav always attributed the success to each member of the team. Even Microsoft CEO Satya Nadella has publicly cited his admiration for Sourav's leadership style. It is no mean feat to receive such admiration from one of the best CEOs globally. When asked about which player's leadership style matched his own, Mr Nadella was quick to respond 'Sourav Ganguly, the unlikely captain from West Bengal' as he too was like him an unlikely CEO of the software giant.* At a tech event for VMware, Sourav shared his leadership mantra in three key factors—identifying the right talent, ensuring the right atmosphere to perform and accepting that every team member is different. In his ability to give opportunities to youngsters, Sourav had this to say at the event:

> Every team should have the right ratio of young and senior or experienced members. The more experienced ones are the best people to guide and help their juniors. The team leader should ensure that it happens. By giving the talent the right opportunity to deliver will only bring success.**

Perhaps it best summarizes his leadership style. There are important lessons to be drawn for every CEO in the above few lines. Sourav's successors, M.S. Dhoni and Virat Kohli, have

---

*https://www.crictracker.com/microsoft-ceo-satya-nadella-feels-sourav-ganguly-will-able-lead-company/
**http://www.cxotoday.com/story/sourav-gangulys-leadership-lessons-for-cxos/

taken the team to newer heights following the same principle. If ever there is a debate on who among them was the best Indian captain, it will not be decided on the number of wins but on the ability to show the team a new direction. Sourav's charismatic leadership achieved the same.

Mental Strength

Successful people have fear, successful people have doubts, and successful people have worries. They just don't let these feelings stop them.

—T. Harv Eker, Canadian author,
businessman and motivational speaker

Most coaches and sports personalities believe that being mentally tough is one of the key ingredients to be successful in any sport. In a technology driven world where every move is analysed, the margin for making an error is reducing every year. In such an environment, thriving competition further ensures that a string of failure can mean the end of the road for any player—one needs to make the most of the limited opportunities that are presented in order to succeed. Cricket is as much a mind game today as it is a field game. With an ever hungry press always ready to report at the slightest hint of controversy, cricketers in India are always under scrutiny. It intensifies in case the team loses and the press forgets entirely that the same players led the team to a remarkable victory few matches ago. In such a situation, Sourav Ganguly emerged as the person who could handle criticism with ease and kept proving his critics wrong. If there ever was a bad boy in Indian cricket who did not mind responding strongly within the country or overseas, it was Sourav. From being tigers at home to emerging as one of the leading sides globally, he instilled in his players the belief and confidence that India could win in any situation. He personally went through various lows in his career and thrived each time under it. What were the factors for his mental strength?

Sourav's ability to believe in himself was the key factor in his making successful comebacks every single time. His brother Snehasish too believes that mental strength is Sourav's greatest weapon. In an interview in 2003, this is what he had to say about his younger brother:

> It's his mental discipline and strength that has taken him where he is today. Mental toughness is Maharaj's (Sourav's nickname) area of strength. He may have seemed subdued at times because of the media glare and the constant pressure to perform, but he has survived because of this quality that allows him to take pressure.*

It is a common trait among great leaders to prove everyone wrong. Elon Musk is a great example for the same—when he started SpaceX hardly anyone believed that he would be able to build commercial rockets. In a similar way, when Steve Jobs returned to lead Apple in 1997, there were few who believed that he could turn around the company in such a short time. While it would be unfair to compare Sourav to Elon Musk or Steve Jobs as they belong to completely unrelated domains,

---

*http://www.rediff.com/cricket/2003/jul/08chayya.htm

there is no denying the fact that he exhibits the same element of mental toughness as these legendary entrepreneurs.

Sourav's mental strength can be analysed using a simple model. His belief in himself is supported by four foundations (Ds): determination, dedication, direction (do it) and delivery. Each of these foundations fuel his sense of purpose and achievement in his goal.

Figure 3.1
Sourav's Belief Model

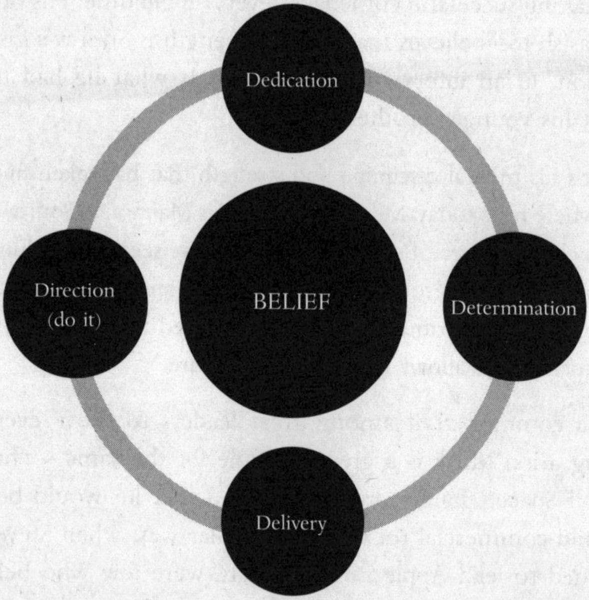

- **Direction:** Sourav believed in doing the task himself; unless he is able to accomplish the task, he will not put unnecessary pressure on any other individual.
- **Determination:** Sourav was determined to make a

comeback to the team and leave on his own terms. Every time he was dropped, he performed and made his way back into the squad.
- **Delivery:** Sourav's focus was also on ensuring that the right results are achieved. His team would comprise of players best suited for a playing condition.
- **Dedication:** Even though many criticized his fitness levels, Sourav used to follow a very stringent fitness regime. During the period when he was dropped from captaincy and the national squad, Sourav was seen practising with a ladder and parachute resistance in order to keep his fitness levels high.

As his belief was based in solid foundation, it did not falter when he was put under pressure time and again. Sourav has always performed exceedingly well when put under pressure. In his debut Test match in Lord's, Sourav was under a lot of pressure mentally to prove his worth in the team. In his biography *A Century Is Not Enough*, Sourav mentions that he used to visualize facing the English bowlers before actually facing the likes of Dominic Cork on the ground. Years later in 1998, under the high-pressure Independence Cup final against Pakistan in Bangabandhu Stadium (Dhaka), Sourav answered with a match-winning 124 runs. This was followed by a knock of 183 in a do-or-die encounter with Sri Lanka in 1999 World Cup. Had it not been for Sourav's knock and his 318-run partnership with Rahul Dravid, India would have been eliminated in the league stages of the tournament. Sourav's real test of his mental strength came to the fore after he was unceremoniously dropped in 2005. Very few could have made a comeback in such a circumstance; yet, Sourav was able to do so.

He has been put under a number of challenging scenarios throughout his career. There are important life lessons that one can draw from each of these incidents. Some of them are:

His International Debut in Australia

Sourav was picked up as a part of India's tour to Australia in 1992 when he was just eighteen years old. Throughout the series he was treated like a co-passenger playing just one game in which he managed to score 3 runs. After this match he was dropped and kept out of the team for the next four years. The series was also remembered due to the controversies surrounding Sourav. It was reported that he was arrogant, refused to carry drinks as the 12th man and had an attitude like a 'Maharaja' (his nickname). While there was no truth in the story and was only an attempt by elements within BCCI to settle scores with the Jagmohan Dalmiya camp, Sourav had to suffer. As a player hailing from the east zone and his family was believed to be close to Jagmohan Dalmiya, he was made to pay the price for no fault of his.

There are few key lessons from this. In offices too, people form groups to gossip about certain employees and these individuals become victims of 'office politics'. It might happen that certain individuals get opportunities one after another whereas few are sidelined after a single failure. In such circumstances, one must retain his or her belief and keep believing that opportunities will knock on their doors in future. If you still feel let down, speak with someone senior in the organization or your mentor for guidance.

> **Learning Tip**
> Life can be unfair sometimes. In moments
> such as those, believe in your abilities.

His First Test Match

Sourav was able to make his debut as Navjot Singh Siddhu had walked out of the team due to differences with the skipper Mohd. Azharuddin. He had made his comeback to the national cricket owing to the strong performances in domestic cricket such as 69 and 65 (for Board President's XI) against England A and unbeaten 200 against Bihar in Ranji Trophy. During the team selection, east zone selector Sambaran Banerjee had proposed Sourav's name looking at his consistency and his bowling abilities which could have helped in seaming conditions in England. Yet, Sourav was considered to get into the team as a quota player who did not merit selection. His centuries in consecutive Tests silenced everyone.

When people question your abilities, work hard and prove them wrong with your performance. You might not succeed in your first attempt, but persevere to achieve your goal and you will definitely get there.

> **Learning Tip**
> Consistent performance is the best
> way to silence your critics.

Marriage with Childhood Sweetheart

Sourav was just 23 when he secretly married his childhood sweetheart. It took a lot of strength to go against one's family at such a young age. The important lesson to learn here is that when it comes to matters of the heart, it is best to follow it. The same is true with our choice of profession—it is best to do what you enjoy doing. This will enable you to always put in the extra effort that is required to succeed.

Learning Tip
Follow your heart in whatever you do in life.

The Rumoured Affair

Indian press had reported that the captain was having an affair with South Indian actress Nagma. While there was no truth in the claims, it did impact the image of Sourav as a family man. In the 2001 series, even the Australian team took advantage of the situation and used it as an instrument for sledging.

In the professional space too, such rumours are often spread in order to malign a person. In such cases the lesser one reacts, the better they are poised to handle it.

Learning Tip
You need to ignore issues which have
no foundation and not react to such reports.

Lord Snooty–County Cricket

During his first stint with County cricket in 2000, Sourav was designated as 'Lord Snooty' by reviewers Steve Pittard and John Stern of the *Wisden Cricketers' Almanack* (the cricket magazine is no longer connected with Wisden and is now known only as *The Cricketer*). The UK telegraph raised several questions on his commitment towards the team and his attitude as he was reportedly busy travelling with his wife instead of being with his teammates. The British dailies repeatedly assaulted him about his career stint with Lancashire. How did Sourav react? He let his performance do the talking for him. In the 2003 World Cup, when India was on a winning spree and reached the finals of the tournament, the same British media hailed him as the captain of the tournament. The *Sunday Observer* wrote in its tabloid, 'For weeks the pundits have praised Ricky Ponting's growing maturity, Stephen Fleming's ingenuity. But Ganguly can lay claim to being the captain of the tournament'.* He returned to UK for two more seasons in 2005 and 2006. Even in the period when he was facing his worst career crisis of being dropped from captaincy and the team in 2005–06, Sourav decided to play in England in order to get some practice in seaming conditions.

Learning Tip
When faced with criticism, the only way
to keep performing is by keeping faith
and being mentally tough

---

*https://timesofindia.indiatimes.com/cricket/From-Lord-Snooty-to-captain-genius-British-media-hails-Ganguly/articleshow/40495323.cms

Being Late for the Toss (India–Australia Series)

You could call it a stroke of luck or pre-planned strategy; it definitely rattled the mind of Australian captain Steve Waugh. It was clearly a case of playing mind games. In another incident during the toss, Sourav was found to be enquiring about the toss result which Steve thought to be claiming the toss. The animosity between the two sides grew to such an extreme level that in the final Test when Steve got out, he was given a send-off by Sourav. Questions were raised over Sourav's conduct, however in the end the strategy proved successful as India won the series 2-1. It was the start of a new rivalry in world cricket which was at par with the Ashes.

- **Six-match ban:** Following this, Sourav faced a six-match ban for his slow over rate in the fourth ODI match against Pakistan in Ahmedabad in 2005. The decision to ban him for six matches was extremely harsh by match referee Chris Broad. Ironically, the BCCI did not appeal against the verdict initially, as the stage was being set for Rahul Dravid to be appointed as the full-time captain. The ban was later reduced to four ODI matches.

  It is important to control one's emotional response to any situation. In fact, it is believed that emotional intelligence is far more important to succeed in our professional career. Sourav could have kept his emotions under check and avoided the criticism. However, in order to build a new Team India, he might have felt this was needed. Imagine a situation where you are able to prove your point in a presentation; will you go about saying the same in the office cubicles? Probably, it will negatively impact your image and people might begin to see you as a self-centred person.

> **Learning Tip**
> Whether in victory or defeat, it is important to keep the emotions under check, otherwise it may lead to unnecessary trouble.

Ganguly–Chappell Controversy

The one incident which probably changed the track of his career was his differences with Greg Chappell. He was stripped off his captaincy and was dropped from the team. Websites such as ihateganguly.com were even launched to further disgrace the skipper which also carried a 'Hate-Ganguly' campaign. Such incidents were not uncommon to him as certain sections of the media had previously targeted him as a non-performing captain. The same papers had also wanted to project Rahul Dravid as the more ideal captain and saw this as an opportunity and take a pro-Chappell stand on the issue. The entire controversy erupted after an email that Chappell had sent to BCCI criticizing Sourav was leaked to media. There is little doubt that many in the establishment wanted him to leave owing his perceived closeness to Jagmohan Dalmiya and were playing the role of puppet masters. The issue was even debated in the parliament as the Left Front MPs demanded his inclusion in the team and protested against the manner in which he was being treated.

Sourav's response to the situation is what makes the story worth remembering. He went back to playing Ranji trophy scoring runs, tried himself for county cricket and when the Indian team's fortune declined, Sourav made his way back into the team. It is easy to fight back when you know that if you perform, you will get another opportunity to be part of the team. However, it is extremely difficult to continue with the fighting spirit when one knows that there are purely non-cricketing reasons behind not allowing someone enter the team. It was his mental toughness and belief in his own abilities that kept him going in such a circumstance. How can any individual build such mental strength? There are some key steps that anyone can follow:

- **Ignore what others say:** The more you ignore, the more you will focus on your performance.
- **Perform for yourself:** Rather than focussing on impressing others or trying to prove them wrong; perform for your self-growth.
- **Self-talk:** Amidst all this negativity, ensure to keep a positive mindset.
- **Two-factor theory:** It is important to have a clear frame of mind in such circumstances by clearly demarcating every issue into two buckets—factors you can control and those you can't. There is nothing worse than over-thinking; it only fills up your mind with lot of issues that do not need your time or effort.
- **Focus on the path:** It is important to focus on the path to be taken rather than the final destination. This will enable you to celebrate smaller milestones and help you stay in the moment.
- **Objective evaluation:** Evaluate each of the steps that you have taken in an objective manner considering all pros and cons along with possible implications and not be guided by emotions. You should look at the situation continuously evaluating your progress and monitoring it daily.

> **Learning Tip**
> When faced with a crisis or severe criticism, believe in yourself.

Slow Batting in World Cup 2007

Sourav was accused of extremely slow batting in the encounter with Bangladesh. He had to play a cautious innings of 66 runs as the Indian top order had fallen quickly in the encounter. The Indian team was given a crushing defeat by Bangladesh in the match, following which it won against Bermuda while losing to Sri Lanka and crashing out of World Cup 2007. Though Sourav emerged as the second-highest run-getter batsman for India, he was singled out for fierce criticism from all quarters by selectors, media and the cricket diaspora at large. He had made a fantastic comeback in the ODI team and was even Man of the Series against Sri Lanka prior to the tournament. Sometimes, individuals are targeted by a single failure. Such occurrences are quite common. In moments such as these, keep chasing your goal.

> **Learning Tip**
> Keep persevering in the face of adversity.

Retirement

Considering his performance over the last three years since his comeback (2005–08), it was quite ironic that Sourav was dropped from the team for the Irani Trophy after just one bad series against Sri Lanka. Sourav, too, in an interview for a Bengali newspaper *Aajkal*, said, 'There is no point playing like this. I am not willing to play at their (selectors') mercy. They will pick you now and then dump you. Why should I be the sacrificial goat all the time? It was difficult to accept.'* Clearly, Sourav was upset about how he had been treated over the years. Yet, when Sourav was selected for the Australia series, the squad was declared for only the first-two Test matches in the four-match series. It was believed that Sourav had been offered an honourable exit and if he did not accept the same, his name will not feature in the last two matches. It was amidst these circumstances that Sourav retired from international cricket and declared the same right before the series. Even former Australian captain Steve Waugh was surprised at this decision considering no one had been groomed to take up his role in the squad. His teammate Sachin Tendulkar too expressed surprise at Sourav's decision. In his last match, Sourav scored a valiant 85 in the first innings and a duck in the second. However, there was still a lot of cricket left in him. Given the circumstances in Indian cricket and him having to prove himself time and again, Sourav must have felt that it was the right time for him to move on.

On the other hand, M.S. Dhoni has been quite calculative and has taken bold decisions regarding his captaincy and retirement from Test cricket. Dhoni left his Test captaincy in December 2014 while continuing with the mantle of ODI and T20 captaincy. Moreover, as Dhoni was already in his thirties, he retired from Test cricket in order to prolong his ODI and T20 career until the World Cup 2019. This enabled Virat Kohli to settle down in the new role as captain for a couple of years before taking on the ODI and T20 captaincy. In a similar manner,

---

*http://www.news18.com/news/india/ganguly-upset-299071.html

one should know when to retire and let others carry on. No one is here to stay permanently. You must know when and how to leave on your own terms.

Learning Tip

Plan your retirement carefully and take a decision based on the situation.

Losing the Captaincy of Kolkata Knight Riders (KKR) (IPL, Season 2)

The controversial multi-captain formula was suggested by KKR coach John Buchanan in order to have a different captain for each field—bowling, batting, fielding and wicketkeeping. In hindsight, it was a process to remove Sourav from captaincy. To make matters worse, the move had the complete support of the KKR management without which Buchanan would not have made such a move. Sourav had led the team from the front in the first season (2008) and had even bagged three Man of the Match awards. Despite being the best captain in the country, he wasn't allowed to lead his own city team in the IPL the next year when it was held in South Africa (2009). The team fared miserably in Season 2 under Brendon McCullum and Sourav led the team again in 2010. The KKR management did not bid for Sourav Season 4 onwards and he eventually retired from IPL leading the Pune franchise in 2012.

Coach for Team India

Recently, Team India needed a coach and Sourav was yet again in the news when Ravi Shastri blamed him for not being selected for the job. In reality the committee for the selection had three members (including Sachin Tendulkar and V.V.S. Laxman), even if Sourav had opposed to the selection, Ravi still could not have been selected. Clearly, it was another instance when Sourav was simply being made the scapegoat.

In our professional sphere too we often cite people who we feel have reached their position through influencing others. Clearly, they must have done something right to reach this far and if presented the right set of opportunities, they would continue to deliver results over and over again. In case of women who have reached the top of the corporate ladder, people tend to find reasons other than her professional capabilities that might have helped her succeed. This is an extremely toxic attitude to possess and will only lead to one's own downfall. If you are good enough for a role that you feel should belong to you, work hard and it will rightfully be yours. Your focus should be on improving yourself rather than criticizing others. It is difficult to break the glass ceiling but if individuals like Kiran Mazumdar Shaw (MD of Biocon), Indra Nooyi (CEO of PepsiCo) and Sundar Pichai (CEO of Google) were able to achieve it, so can you! It is only a matter of belief and perfect execution that sets and builds the difference between any two individuals.

Learning Tip

It is our performance and skills that support us in breaking the glass ceiling and ensuring success.

For someone who had handled so many controversies and been tested numerous times in his career, Sourav definitely symbolizes exceptional mental strength. In order to be mentally tough like Sourav, we need to think like him. According to Cough, Earle and

Sewell,* there are several traits which are associated with being mentally strong. They created a triangle showcasing the traits that are common across mentally-strong people. In the analysis below, Sourav's traits have been analysed using the same model.

Figure 3.2
Sourav's Traits for Mental Toughness Based on Clough, Earle and Sewell's Concept

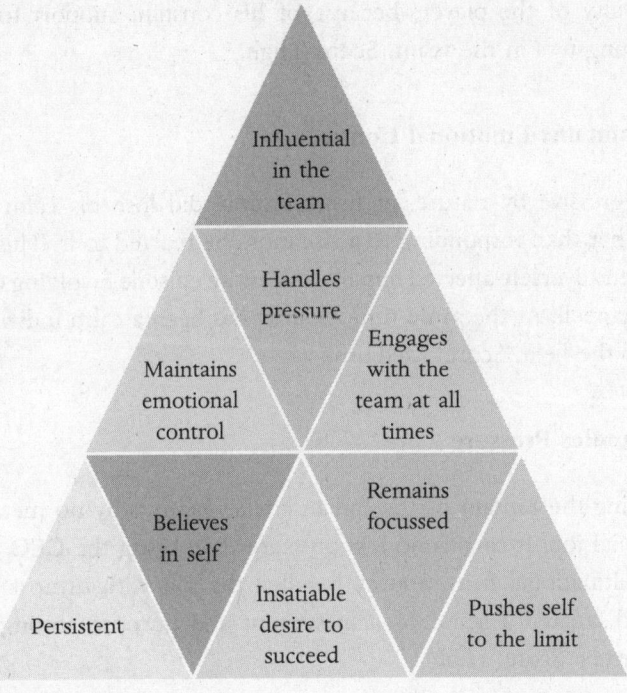

---

*P.J. Clough, K. Earle and D. Sewell. 2002. *Mental Toughness: The Concept and Its Measurement*. London: Thomson Learning.

If we consider the characteristics of Sourav and rate him based on each of these criteria as high, medium or low, we will find a strong reason for his mental toughness.

Influential in the Team

As captain of the team that he had built from scratch, Sourav was definitely an influential person. Moreover, Sourav had the loyalty of the players because of his constant support to the youngsters in the team. Score: High!

Maintains Emotional Control

Aggressive by nature, at times Sourav did lose his calm and rather than responding to a situation, he reacted to it. This has even adversely affected him like the entire episode involving Greg Chappell. At the same time, Sourav has been a calm individual off the field. Score: Medium!

Handles Pressure

Being the captain of the Indian cricket team is by no means a trivial job. It carries no less pressure than being the CEO of a multinational firm. Sourav handled the job with utmost ease and created a sense of achievement and purpose among the players. Score: High!

Engages with the Team

Sourav was always involved in the game whether through batting, bowling or field placements. His ability to motivate players during the game is well-known. Even after retirement, Sourav continues to be strongly associated with the game. Score: High!

Persistence

Sourav continued with his strategy to perform well in domestic cricket when all seemed lost. Moreover, he equally persisted with youngsters and gave them a fair number of opportunities to prove themselves. Score: Medium

Believes in Self

This was perhaps the only reason for his successful comebacks. Sourav definitely had loads of it. Score: High!

Insatiable Desire to Succeed

Sourav was clear that he wanted to play cricket for Team India and do well at the international level. This in turn made him perform and train harder. Even when he retired from international cricket, he could have continued with his insatiable desire to succeed. Score: High!

Remains Focussed

Sourav's focus on winning matches for the country was one of the key reasons for winning on overseas tracks. Rather than settling for a draw, he was able to make the team focus for a win. Score: High!

Pushes Self to the Limit

Sourav doesn't need any introduction for this. He has pushed himself to the wall and bounced back. He wasn't the quickest on the field, but there was no lack in the efforts. Score: High!

Out of the nine criteria in the triangle, Sourav scores high in seven fields. With Sourav, it was not about the amount of runs that he managed to score, it wasn't the ability to win matches, it wasn't the controversies, but it was his mental strength that made him stand apart from the rest of cricketers. One day when the dust will finally settle down, people will look up to Sourav for who he was—a sportsperson with impeccable mental strength who played to win.

Quick Learner

There are no secrets to success. It is the result of preparation, hard work and learning from failure.

—Colin Powell, former US Secretary of State

How important is it to learn a skill at a fast pace? In today's environment, coupled with technological advances, our lives have become a function of how we spend our time. Time is the only limited resource and in many ways, how we utilize it defines who we become. Man in his quest of developing machines has begun the race to become a machine himself. Sports, too, are not untouched by the technological advances. Each time a cricketer takes on to the field, there are hundreds of analysts recording his moves, strengths and weaknesses. It seems as if the bowler knows where to bowl the next time the batsman comes to batting crease and he will surely lose his wicket. However, this is not the case, as good players are consistently thinking out of the box and working on their weak points. In their quest to perfect themselves, they are consistently working on their fitness levels and developing new skills. Yahoo is a classic example of a company which did not quickly learn from its mistakes. The company missed an opportunity to buy out Google for just 1 million USD and lost the search engine war to the same company later. Google too lost in the race of social media networking to Facebook and Twitter. In business and technology, a company's ability to adapt at an extremely quick pace makes all the difference between being dominant and oblivious.

A similar parallel can be drawn from the field of finance as well. Being a hyper competitive industry, individuals are constantly upgrading their skills to be better in the field by working on challenging assignments, undertaking various certifications or attending different types of workshops. In today's world the ideology is quite simple—improve or perish.

If we consider the cricketer Sourav Ganguly, he has grown from strength to strength each time he has taken to the field. Let us look at his childhood days when he was passionate about playing football. Coming from a family with strong connections to cricket, he eventually switched over to cricket. His father was associated with the CAB as secretary and chairman of the board of trustees. Cricket, therefore, was deeply rooted in his genes. His brother Snehashish Ganguly too played Ranji cricket for Bengal. But is it easy to change your passion from one game to another? The answer is a definite no. The case is very similar to a professional working in the marketing division being asked to perform tasks for someone in the financial department. It is by no means a simple task. In circumstances like these our adaptability to the situation comes into picture—whether we can mould ourselves according to the situation or not. During a media session for the Indian Soccer League where Sourav is the co-owner of ATK, he was candid enough to admit the same by saying the following:

> My first memories of football were my first memories of a sport. Because I never played cricket when I was young, I used to kick the football. Studying in St Xavier's, after 3 p.m. it was football for me and I didn't know what a cricket bat was although my brother used to play cricket.*

It is not easy to add a new skill and succeed in life especially when it comes to excelling at the international level in a hypercompetitive sport like cricket. Yet, for someone who did not play the game, to go on to lead the country speaks volumes about the capabilities of the person. Among cricketers, only A.B. de Villiers comes to mind as having passion for multiple sports such as tennis and has been ranked nationally no. 1 in his age group a few times. Sourav, who was a right-handed player, started using his left hand so that he could use his brother's kit. He had this uncanny habit of adapting to the situation at a very young age. It is this adaptability that served him in good stead to emerge as one of the finest left-handed batsmen to have played the game.

Adaptability can simply be looked at as a personality trait that determines how we respond to change. High adaptability means more chances of succeeding in business. A valid example in this case is that of Nokia which at its peak controlled more than 70 per cent of all mobile phones being sold worldwide. It was the first company that was approached by Google to introduce Android in its smartphones. Yet, Nokia being complacent did not feel the need to change and perished eventually and finally was sold out to Microsoft. Later, it licensed its brand name to HMD Global. Adaptability also helps in ensuring a foresighted

---

*http://www.goal.com/en-india/news/136/india/2014/08/02/4999164/as-a-young-boy-it-was-all-about-watching-football-sourav

vision for any firm. For instance, when it came to adapting to the changes with the advent of digital photography, Kodak failed miserably and lost its dominance in the market. Kodak was slow to transform its film-based business to a more technology-oriented digital mode and by the time it realised this, it was too late.

In the book *The Platinum Rule*, authors Tony Alessandra and Michael O'Connor describes adaptability comprising of two key components: flexibility and versatility. Flexibility refers to how receptive we are to change, whereas versatility means how skilfully we function at different levels. In short, it is a combination of our attitude and ability. If we try to plot Sourav on this graph of attitude vs ability, he will lie above the 45-degree line. Sourav may have not been the most talented cricketer, but he was quick to modify himself according to the situation, work towards the change and continuously improve.

Figure 4.1
Sourav Ganguly vs Other Players: Adaptability Graph

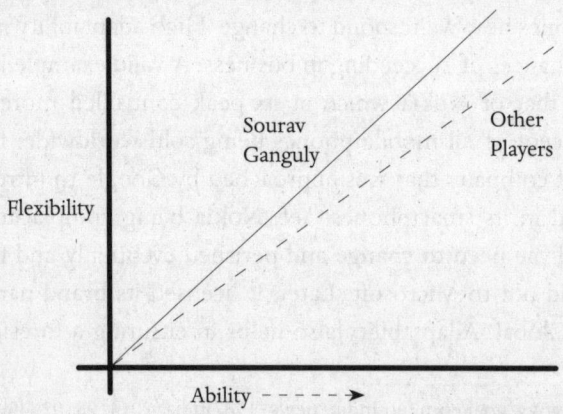

Sourav made his debut in seaming English conditions and made his mark in international cricket by scoring centuries in his first-two Test matches. It is not a normal thing for batsmen from a sub-continent to do well in seaming conditions, considering they are brought up in flat spinning tracks. However, for Sourav, there was no other way; his opportunity with the national side had come to him after four long years and if he did not perform well, it could have been the end of his cricketing career. Sourav decided to apply his skills to the maximum and decimated the English attack becoming the only Indian to score a century in the debut match at Lord's till date. If we consider the skills of other players in the team, players like Sachin and Azharuddin had more experience, yet it was Sourav's adaptability that made the difference. Years later, Sourav showed the same determination in his performance against Pakistan scoring consistently over the years—in Brisbane (2003) scoring 144 runs and his comeback to international cricket in pace-friendly South African tracks (2006) scoring 51 was instrumental in ensuring the Test victory. If we try to look at the characteristics of Sourav as a player, his ability to learn quickly has made significant differences to the chances of the team.

Sourav's quick learning abilities helped him in several ways:

Becoming Valuable to the Team

Sourav's ability to bat at any position made him an extremely valuable asset in the team. He could open the batting or play in the middle order in both Test matches and One-Day cricket. In fact, he has batted in all positions—from 1 to 6—in international cricket. He was no less effective in bowling with 100 ODI wickets and 32 Test wickets. While his bowling was often overlooked, it was his all-round abilities that got him his first Man of the Series in the Sahara Cup against Pakistan. He remained an integral part of the team in both forms of the game for the larger part of his illustrious career.

Similarly, in today's corporate career, individuals who have multiple skills are highly valued in any profession. Having diversified skills enable an individual to think creatively and come up with out-of-the-box solutions to complex problems.

Improving Leadership Skills

Captaincy was thrust on Sourav Ganguly in the midst of the match-fixing controversy, which engulfed several key players in the team. It was out there that Sourav's quick learning abilities came to the rescue as he took the team from strength to strength. He was willing to experiment, analyse the pitch conditions and pick the side that was best suited to win the game. As captain, he had to analyse the playing situation and act accordingly at every point of time. A case in point is the 2001 Eden Gardens Test with Australia in the Border–Gavaskar trophy when Sourav asked Sachin to bowl. Australia were at 161/3 and were poised to save the Test when Sachin picked up two quick wickets of Adam Gilchrist and Mathew Hayden. The rest they say is history as India became the third team to beat a side after following on. Sourav was quick to understand that Harbhajan needed a spinning partner to break the Australian partnership and Sachin seemed the perfect fit to the situation. During his cricketing career, as captain of the side, his field placements and bowling changes stand testimony to his quick learning abilities and is regarded as one of the greatest captains to have ever played the game.

Imagine a situation on the trading floor when a stock is crashing, how quickly can you react to the situation? It is your agility in those situations that will make the difference between winning and losing any corporate battle.

Satisfaction in Life

Being flexible and adapting to change brings up a lot of possibilities in life. For instance, when Sourav was often criticized for his weakness against the short-pitched deliveries, he used his ability to quickly learn and overcome the same. I do find the criticism to be a bit overhyped as hardly any batsman in world cricket enjoys playing the short ball. However, if Sourav had not overcome his weakness, there is little doubt that he would not have been able to play international cricket for over a decade. 18,000+ international runs stand testimony to this fact. It was his ability to apply his mind in the playing crease that made the difference. His skill sets were incomparable in the offside as he could pierce any field with his explosive batting. Even after retirement, Sourav has been quick to adapt to life beyond cricket.

Managing Career Transitions

Sourav is one of the few cricketers who have been able to make a smooth transition to life beyond cricket. He has been quick to emerge as a skilful cricket administrator—president of CAB. There have been few cricketers who have had successful careers as administrators. His decisions with respect to renovating Eden Gardens or standing up for domestic Ranji players' pay hikes imply that Sourav has quickly transcended to the role. He is also arguably the wittiest and most analytical commentators in the current period. His insightful analyses of match situations prove the sharp cricketing brain that he possesses. He also hosts several game shows on television and has equally succeeded as a popular anchor on local Bengali television. For someone who can do well in such unrelated challenging roles, there is little doubt that he would be an extremely sharp individual. Depending on the situation he moulds himself and succeeds under any circumstance.

Ability to Make Comebacks

The art of making comebacks is largely dependent on learning from mistakes and reinventing oneself according to the changed situation. When Sourav had returned to the Indian team after being dropped from the side and was targetted unfairly by the coach, he was a completely different batsman in utterly hostile conditions. In addition to this, the dressing room atmosphere was not particularly conducive for someone making a comeback. Yes, mental strength does play a part here, but to adapt to such conditions is equally important.

If we consider the corporate history, there have been quite a few known personalities who have made successful comebacks. Walt Disney was fired from Kansas City Star as its editor felt that he wasn't creative enough. He eventually went on to create Mickey Mouse and ultimately built one of the largest studios in the world. Michael Bloomberg was fired from Salomon Brothers when it was acquired by Citi. He went on to start Bloomberg with his severance package and became one of the richest persons in the world. The list is endless and Sourav certainly belongs to the same list.

Bad things happen to all of us. It could be an accident, being fired from a job, a broken marriage or a death in the family. Sourav was no exception to the rule. If you are resilient, you will take adversity in your stride and march ahead. Circumstances such as these should only make your resolve stronger to face newer problems the very next day.

Presence of Mind

Being a quick learner, Sourav is extremely witty in his response in several occasions. In his commentating career, we have been able to witness several such situations. For instance, in the penultimate Test match with Sachin Tendulkar at Eden Gardens, Harsha Bhogle had asked him quite categorically if Sachin would be more popular than Sourav during the match. Sourav responded in an extremely witty manner by suggesting that only for those five days of the match Sachin would be popular. It is his sharp mind and the ability to react in a sporty manner that set him aside from the rest. As skipper, Sourav was used to facing the media glare which helped him learn the tricks of facing the camera—saying exactly what needs to be told in the most sublime manner. He brought the same skills in his career as a commentator.

As a player who had hardly played any T20 cricket, Sourav did exceptionally well in his first season with Kolkata Knight Riders bagging three Man of the Match awards. The team narrowly missed the semi-final spot and Sourav had to be content without lifting the trophy. His ability to learn from the past and make amends is a model to behold. Sourav follows a simple mechanism to boost his abilities which we can all follow:

- **Learn from the experience of others:** Even when Sourav was not playing cricket at the international level, he made it a point to watch every international game being played at the Eden Gardens. By observing how different skippers adapted according to conditions and executed their strategies, Sourav was able to learn some of the tricks of captaincy when he was very young. When Sourav became a part of the national team and later the captain, he had the benefit of the likes of Kumble and Tendulkar in the dressing room. By facilitating an open culture, Sourav was able to create an experience of sharing the knowledge across the team where people were not afraid to air their views. This exponentially benefitted the youngsters who could garner a lot from the experience of the seniors.

- **Plan the activities:** Sourav's learning was driven by the outcome whether it was practising at the nets or following a stringent fitness regime, his desire to represent the country kept him going. This in turn enabled him to plan the activities needed to achieve his dream and focus on the desired outcome.
- **Evaluate the lessons learnt and be prepared to unlearn:** Whether it is evaluating a business plan or making a bowling change, one must be ready to adapt according to the situation. Similarly, individuals and professionals must always be willing to learn new skills and adapt ourselves to the change. Twists and turns in anyone's life is common; it is how we understand and respond to the situation is what makes the difference.

Food for thought: Are you investing as an organization in the learning of your employees to use as a competitive weapon?

People are the most critical resource in today's environment. It is of utmost importance that organizations hire individuals who are quick to grasp new skills, emerge as thinkers and believe in flawless execution. Just like sports, individuals who are slow to adapt to change will perish in the long run. In the words of Arie De Gus, a business theorist: 'The ability to learn faster than your competitors may be the only sustainable competitive advantage.' Perhaps, it is the same reason why Sourav Ganguly could play such an important role in shaping Indian cricket.

Sourav's Best Cricketing Innings

With over 18,000 international runs, Sourav Ganguly is undoubtedly one of the greatest captains and players to have played for India. This section looks at some of his best innings and the lessons that we can draw from each of the situations. The innings have been lined up in chronological order.

- **131 vs England, Lord's, 20–24 June 1996:** In his debut Test match, Sourav was under tremendous pressure to make this opportunity count. It is significant to note that this opportunity came after almost 4 years of his international debut in 1992. Sourav was unceremoniously dropped following questions about his attitude.

    In a match where England had scored 344 in the first innings, the Indian innings started poorly with India losing their first wicket of Vikram Rathour and the score at 25/1. It was at this moment that Sourav came to the crease and played arguably one of the best innings of his life. While wickets tumbled at the other end, he held on to his own and ensured that the score kept ticking on. His 131 run knock included 20 boundaries as he single-handedly kept questioning the English attack. Sourav's composure awed the audience at Lord's who gave a standing ovation when he departed from the crease. Sourav also bowled 18 overs in the match, conceding 54 runs and picking up 3 wickets including those of Nasser Hussain and Graeme Hick in the match. He followed it up with another century in the next match at Trent Bridge.

Years later, this is how Sourav recollected his emotions of playing for the country in a Test match:

> We were staying in a hotel just opposite Lord's. We walked down to the ground and Azhar told me that I was in. It was a great moment in my life.*

Sourav, in the process, became the 62nd batsman and the 10th Indian player to score a century on their Test debut. He also became the third player to score a century on debut at Lord's. (The feat was also achieved by Harry Graham [1893], John Hampshire [1969] and Andrew Strauss [2004]). The opportunity to play for the country came after lot of hardships and Sourav made the most of it with his grit and determination. Sometimes we too face a challenging situation at our workplace or are allotted an assignment beyond our comfort zone. It is in moments like these that we actually are tested.

Learning tip

Make the most of the opportunities and keep performing when it matters the most.

---

*http://www.news18.com/cricketnext/news/rewind-1996-the-debuts-to-remember-575729.html

- **75* vs Pakistan, Sahara Cup, Toronto, 20 September 1997:** There are few rivalries bigger than India and Pakistan in world cricket and Sourav chose the stage to prove his value in the Indian team. Set in the city of Toronto, the series was dubbed as the friendship series between the two arch rivals. Sourav excelled in the series both with his batting and bowling bagging four consecutive Man of the Match awards in an ODI series (a world record still held by Sourav). Sourav scored a total of 222 runs in the series with scores of 17, 32, DNB, 2, 75* and 96. He bagged 15 wickets at an average of under 11 runs, proving to be Pakistan's nemesis with India winning the series 4-1. His 75 unbeaten run-a-ball knock was extremely significant since India was given a total of 160 runs to chase in 26 overs in the rain-hit match. During the chase, India was tottering at 54-3 having lost Sachin Tendulkar, Robin Singh and Mohd. Azharuddin. It was at this moment that Sourav was joined by Ajay Jadeja (37*) in an unbeaten 108-run partnership and helped India take a 4-0 lead in the series.

In corporate life too at times, we need to deliver results within a very short time. It is on such occasions that our work determines our growth and ascent in a team. Our performance at those junctures helps in gaining the trust of our superiors and ensures that we are considered for critical assignments in future.

Learning Tip

Consistent performance in challenging situations is what defines us in corporate life.

- **89 vs Pakistan, Karachi, 30 September 1997:** The innings was significant as it came right after the Sahara Cup where Sourav had single-handedly demolished the Pakistani side. More so because Sourav had been dismissed for a duck in the previous innings. Sourav scored a match-winning 89 runs for 96 balls and provided the much-needed momentum for the Indian team to take on the Pakistani total. His innings comprised of 11 fours against arguably one of the best bowling line-ups. It was also the time when Sourav was slowly beginning to eclipse the performances of Sachin Tendulkar and emerging as India's best match-winner in any situation. Having set a target of 266 to win, by the time Sourav departed, he had already set India on course to a famous win. This win was special as it was Sourav's first tour to Pakistan and considering the hostilities between the two countries; nothing could have been more special than scoring a match-winning knock on Pakistani turf.
- **124 vs Pakistan, Independence Cup, Dhaka, 18 January 1998:** Arguably, this innings signified that India had finally found another player at the top of the order who could carry the mantle of leading India to a victory in the absence of Sachin Tendulkar. India had long been a one-man army with Sachin carrying the burden of the country's expectations. Pakistan scored a mammoth 314 runs in the final at Banga Bandhu Stadium led by a brilliant 140 by Pakistani opener Saeed Anwar. In a high intensity final amidst the presence of cricket-loving Bangladeshi crowd, the total of 314 seemed no less than 350 against a bowling line-up comprising Saqlain Mushtaq, Aaqib Javed and Azhar Mahmood.

    India had a good start with Sachin scoring a quick-fire 41

before departing. It was at this juncture that Sourav started playing the anchor role scoring a brilliant 124 comprising of 11 fours and 1 six. Along with Robin Singh, the duo stitched together a 189-run partnership taking the score nearer to the target. By the time, Sourav departed the score was at 274-4 before Hrishikesh Kanitkar and Javagal Srinath ensured that India sailed through in an absolute thriller.

It was Sourav Ganguly's third ODI century and the first in a high-pressure final against Pakistan. There was no looking back for him from this point onwards as he had proven himself as a big-match player who can handle pressure with ease.

It is arguably one of those innings which defined Sourav's ODI career.

- **183 vs Sri Lanka, ICC World Cup, 26 May 1999:** There are few innings in the history of World Cups where a single player has demolished the defending champion with his stroke play and unflinching attack from the start. Sourav along with Rahul Dravid (145) stitched together a 318-run partnership to set a target of 374 runs. Sri Lanka in response could only manage 216 runs and lost the match by 157 runs. Sourav's innings of 183 came in just 158 deliveries and comprised of 17 fours and 1 towering six. On that day, Sourav was simply unassailable. It was as if the 'God of Offside' was destined to ensure that Sri Lankans would not be able to defend their title. The Sri Lankan bowling attack consisted of legends like Chaminda Vaas and Muttiah Muralitharan, and yet he was unstoppable. It remains the third-highest individual score in the World Cup history after Chris Gayle (215 vs Zimbabwe, WC 2015) and Garry Kristen (188* vs UAE, WC 1996). While the other two scores came against minnows, Sourav's innings came against the defending world champion.

Sourav batted through the innings and was only dismissed in the 50th over in what can be described as one of the best ODI innings ever. India desperately needed to win the match to stay in the competition and Ganguly rose to the occasion to deliver the necessary outcome.

Learning Tip

In order to become the best in any profession, you need to rise to occasion when the situation demands it.

- **141* vs South Africa, ICC Knockout, 13 October 2000:** Captain Sourav was now at the helm of affairs leading the country into the first ICC event in his tenure. The tournament was significant as it came right after the match-fixing controversy with several Indian players, including former skipper Mohd. Azharuddin, under the scanner. It was important that the faith of the game be restored in the minds of the general public. This further pressurized the new captain.

  Sourav batted right through the innings once more with an unbeaten 141 of 142 balls, studded with 11 fours and 6 sixes. He was ably supported during the match by Sachin Tendulkar (39), Rahul Dravid (58) and Yuvraj Singh (41) to post a challenging total of 295-6. By setting a score of 296 to win, the South Africans could not handle the pressure and crumbled to a total of 200 runs, ensuring India moved to the finals to take on New Zealand. The clash was even more significant as both India and South Africa had been hit hard by the match-fixing controversy post the Hansie Cronje episode. It was a battle of pride and rebuilding two teams and Captain Sourav ensured that India came out on top.

In one of the first tournaments as captain, Sourav earned the respect of his team members by leading from the front and with his own performance. It was the beginning of a new glorious period for the team and the birth of 'Team India' under his leadership.

Leaders lead by example. Whether it is Bill Gates or former US President Obama, people respect them for their conduct both in their personal and professional lives. In a similar manner, the events are no different in the cricketing field—in order to command respect among your teammates, first you need to perform on the field and be worthy of the team cap. Sourav had done just that.

Learning Tip

In order to be a successful leader,
you have to lead from the front.

- **98* (2nd Innings) vs Sri Lanka, Kandy, 22–25 August 2001:** This innings was extremely significant considering the fact that Sourav's performance had begun to suffer post his ascent to captaincy in Test cricket. Prior to this innings, his last fifty had come 13 innings ago. In fact, few would have believed that Sourav would be able to stage such a magnificent match winning innings.

  Yet, once again, Sourav decided to prove his critics wrong. He guided the team to victory and ensured that the series ended at 1-1. His knock came in just 152 deliveries and comprised of 15 boundaries against a bowling line-up comprising the guile of Muttiah Muralitharan.

It is rightfully said that circumstances do not portray an individual as weak or strong, but it shows the person's inner strength to believe in his abilities. It is the belief coupled with hard work that ensures success for an individual in any field.

Learning Tip

Believe in your abilities when others start doubting it.
It is the only way to ensure your success.

- **60 vs England, Lord's, Natwest Trophy Final, 13 July 2002:** The Natwest Trophy final will undoubtedly be regarded as one the best ODI games of all times. Set a challenging total of 326 to win, India were struggling at 146/5 before Yuvraj Singh and Mohammad Kaif ensured a near impossible Indian victory. At that juncture, few would have believed that such a chase was possible by a young Indian side. However, it was the emergence of Team India under Sourav that was responsible for the favourable outcome. Sourav's quick and valuable 60 runs at the top of the order ensured that India, despite losing wickets, was always in pace with the run rate. Sourav celebrated in style by taking off his shirt at the Lord's balcony and showing the world his passion as a leader.

  Virender Sehwag recollected the moment years later in a tweet:

  14 years ago on this day we won the NatWestSeries & @SGanguly99 did a Salman Khan & won everyone's hearts.#NewIndia – July 13, 2016

The match was significant in more ways than one. It ensured in highlighting that Team India was now a force to reckon with and was no longer a one-man army. It also highlighted that Sourav's faith in youngsters was beginning to bear fruit as two of them were primarily responsible for ensuring the victory. When a team has a captain who leads from the front and believes in their abilities, the team rises to the occasion.

Learning Tip

If you believe in your team members and their abilities,
it is only a matter of time before they start
delivering results.

- **128 (1st Innings) vs England, Leeds, 22–26 August 2002:** It was on a seaming track at Leeds that Sourav decided to bat first. Being 1-0 down in the series, India desperately needed to win to ensure that the series stayed alive. Thankfully, opener Sanjay Bangar and Rahul Dravid laid a strong foundation with a 170-run stand for the second wicket, followed by a 150-run partnership between Dravid and Tendulkar. Once Dravid departed, Sourav joined Sachin on the crease with the score at 335-3. They shared a 249-run partnership with Sourav contributing 128 in the partnership before being bowled by Alex Tudor. India posed a massive 628 for 7 before declaring their first innings. The score proved insurmountable for the English team and they managed to score just 273 (1st innings) and 309 (2nd innings) losing the match by an innings and 46 runs.

    Sourav's innings comprised of 14 boundaries and 3

towering sixes, which ensured an important overseas victory for the Indian team, levelling the series at 1-1.

- **107* vs Kenya , Cape Town, World Cup 2003, 7 March 2003:** While this innings might have come up against a minnow, it was extremely important to ensure the Indian victory against a resurgent Kenyan side. Chasing 226 runs to win, India were tottering at 26/3 after 10 overs having lost both the openers Sachin Tendulkar and Virender Sehwag along with Mohd. Kaif in the Super Six game. It was at this juncture that Sourav steadied the innings first with Rahul Dravid (32) followed by Yuvraj Singh (58*). Sourav batted right till the end in his unbeaten knock of 107 comprising 11 fours and 2 sixes. India went on to play the finals of the World Cup, where they lost to defending champions Australia.

- **144 (1st Innings) vs Australia, Brisbane, 4–8 December 2003:** Sourav Ganguly was never quite regarded as a Test batsman in comparison to his achievements as an ODI batsman. Moreover, he had never scored a century against Australia prior to this innings. Yet, on that day, Sourav decided to defy the odds in an innings that completely redefined his stature as a Test batsman. Australia batted first and were bowled out for 323 in the first innings. In response, Sourav came to bat with India reeling at 62/3 having lost Sehwag, Dravid and Tendulkar. In such a situation had Sourav failed, it would have resulted in another defeat. Instead, his defiant and attacking 144 ensured that India leads with 86 runs in the first innings. The match resulted in a draw with Australia declaring at 284 for 3 and India scoring 73/2 before the match was officially declared as drawn. It was the first time that a visiting team had managed to take lead in the first innings in recent memory and was questioning the hegemony of Australian side. Sourav's innings set the tone for the entire series which ended at 1-1 and marked the beginning of the India–Australia rivalry in world cricket.

- **51* vs South Africa at Johannesburg, 15–19 December 2006:** What happens when all the cricket pundits, experts, commentators and even the coach decide to question the attitude and calibre of a player like Sourav? He responds by making a comeback to the same side and scoring a match winning 51 not out in a low-scoring game. Sourav came to the crease with the team at 110/4 and batted right through the innings even stitching a 44-run partnership for the last wicket with V.R.V. Singh taking the Indian total to 249 in the first innings. The match was extremely significant as it meant he was able to prove his critics wrong.

  In response, South Africa were bowled out for just 84 with a magical bowling spell of 5 for 40 from S. Sreesanth. In response, India scored 236 in the second innings setting the Proteas a target of 402 to win. The South African team was eventually bowled out for 272 losing the match by 130 runs. Sourav's innings ensured that Team India had an invaluable lead in the first innings.

  The innings was a reflection of Sourav's mental toughness and resilience to face any adverse situation. It was a hallmark of a great sportsperson and his ability to make his performance do the talking.

Learning Tip

Life will throw several challenges at you. It is your mental strength and perseverance that will show you the way through these circumstances.

- **98 vs West Indies, Nagpur, 21 January 2007:** Having proven his point in the Test series against South Africa, Sourav finally made his comeback in the ODI team after almost 16 months. He responded with a match-winning knock of 98 which showed that he was firmly in control of the shorter version of the game and the hunger and desire for runs never diminished. It was unfortunate that he was run-out with just 2 short of a dominating century. However, his innings had already proven the critics wrong. His 110-ball knock comprised of 11 fours and 3 sixes. Though the West Indian batting was fully-supported by a strong response led by Shivnarine Chanderpaul (149) and Chris Gayle (52), they eventually fell short by 14 runs.
- **239 vs Pakistan, Bangalore (now Bengaluru), 8–12 December 2007:** Sourav's maiden double century came against arch rival Pakistan in Bengaluru in December. It is ironic that the innings came at the end of his career. However, it showed that the 'Maharaja' still had the same hunger and passion for the game. His 239-run knock consisted of 30 boundaries and 2 sixes and was truly reminiscent of the Sourav at Lord's during his debut.

    Aided by the performance and centuries from Yuvraj Singh and Irfan Pathan, India managed to post a massive total of 626 runs in the first innings. Sourav came to bat with the score at 44/2 and by the time he was dismissed by Danish Kaneria, India had sailed past 600 runs. Pakistan too responded well by scoring 537 runs. India declared their second innings at 284 for 6, which included a 91 from Sourav's bat, setting Pakistan a target of 374 runs in the fourth innings. Pakistan lost 7 wickets in their response. However, they managed to save the match. Sourav scored a total of 330 runs in the match and also picked up a wicket. Even at 35, Sourav was still proving himself again and again.

Learning Tip

It is the desire to succeed that makes the difference between success and failure. Age and not performance should always be the criteria to measure a person.

Amidst all the innings, there were two aspects in common—Sourav's passion for the game and his desire to win. He might not have been the most gifted player, but through his sheer belief and commitment, he has always been able to prove his critics wrong. When people and cricket pundits had written him off, Sourav maintained that he will not give up without a fight and will win back his place in the team through his performance.

If you step into his shoes, after having scored more than 15,000 runs in international cricket, how would you have felt to be stripped off captaincy and then your place in the team? At 34 years, even age was not on his side. Yet, he believed in himself when everyone else designated him as a spent force.

There is so much to learn from Sourav's life for any young professional. Even if sometimes we perform to the best of our abilities, the results are not immediately reflected at our workplace. There might be situations when despite our efforts, someone else gets promoted to a position which is rightfully ours. Should we then give up? We should keep working hard to ensure that we keep adding on to our skill set so that we are ready when the right opportunity comes our way.

Sourav's career span teaches us exactly the same. If we look at the career of any sportsperson, it will look very similar to a product lifecycle curve. (A product lifecycle curve looks at the various stages that it goes through—introduction, adoption, peak and decline). In case of Sourav, he just keeps re-inventing himself and rises each time like a phoenix. It is almost like each time you write him off, it only makes him more determined.

Risk Taker

The biggest risk is not taking any risk... In a world that's changing really quickly, the only strategy that is guaranteed to fail is not taking risks.

—Mark Zuckerberg, Co-founder of Facebook

Risk can lead us to a situation where we are exposed to an unfavourable outcome. This outcome could be a consequence of our actions or owing to forces beyond our control. Yet, while none of us favour taking risks, it is an inherent story of the progress of mankind in any sphere. If there was no risk involved in launching rockets in outer space, everyone would have become Elon Musk. It is owing to the risk involved in any task that few dare to take and even fewer actually succeed in accomplishing the mission. In fact, both of Musk's companies (Tesla and SpaceX) were on the verge of bankruptcy when things turned around for the futurist entrepreneur. Building the future comes at a cost that few are willing to take. Cricket as a sport is no different. Unlike individual sports like tennis, cricket being a team sport increases the risks manifold. In the field of finance, assets in an investment portfolio are chosen if the overall risk of the portfolio is less than the sum of the risk level of individual assets. Now consider an 11-asset portfolio where an active portfolio manager is consistently trying out newer combinations to extract the best returns in the market. These assets are similar to players on the field and the portfolio manager is the captain who is consistently looking at maximizing the potentials of his resources. That portfolio of assets is the Indian cricket team and its manager is Sourav Ganguly.

Sourav's tryst with taking risks can be seen even in his personal life. After returning from the English tour, Sourav eloped with his childhood sweetheart and got married in a style reminiscent of Bollywood. He was just 23 years old then. As their families were against the marriage, he convinced Dona Ganguly (then Roy) that this would perhaps be the only way to convince their parents. After getting their marriage registered, they returned to their respective houses as if nothing had happened and kept the matter a secret for six long months. The families had been business partners at one point of time. However, owing to disputes in their business they had fallen apart.* Once the news was disclosed to the families, they had little option but to agree to the union of the two lovers. Sourav and Dona eventually had a grand wedding in February 1997 much to the delight of fans all over the world. Sourav was quite calculative in taking the risk as he felt that it would be the right approach to reunite the two families. He then ensured that the matter be kept under wraps to avoid unnecessary attention from the media. Clearly, it was a combination of risk along with the right strategy in place in his personal life as well. Marriage, they say is the biggest risk to encounter, yet Sourav

---

*https://www.indiatimes.com/sports/sourav-ganguly-s-love-story-with-wife-dona-is-bound-to-give-you-relationship-goals-325296.html

had prospered in the same as well.

Learning Tip

Being able to judge and determine the optimum level of risk that should be taken is often the difference between success and failure.

When in crisis, it is our ability to remain calm and composed that makes all the difference. Imagine a stressful situation at your workplace; would you resign as you find the pressure too much to handle? The key to success in almost every field lies in taking well-calculated risks. If we look at the risk-to-reward ratio, with increasing risk, the rewards will increase. However, the probability of success will decrease accordingly. It is out here that we should look at creating an optimum balance between risk and chances of success.

**Figure 5.1
Risk-Return Curve for Optimal Risk Level**

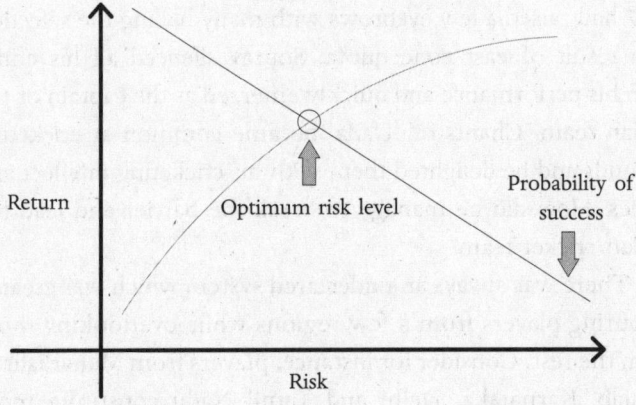

Let us try to analyse the same in terms of cricket. As captain, Sourav had to choose the playing 11, each time weighing the risks taken compared to the chances of winning the encounter. Sourav took over the team at the time when the match-fixing controversy was at its peak. The confidence of the team was running low as senior cricketers like Mohd Azharuddin, Ajay Jadeja and Nayan Mongia had been dragged into the controversy and Sachin Tendulkar had resigned as the captain in 2000 paving the way for a new leadership. Clearly, the risk factor for Sourav was manifold. On one hand, he had to build a team and restore the faith of the common man in Indian cricket with the help of youngsters. The lack of experience among this talented bunch was a risk he had to cater to. On the other hand, being the Indian captain implied that now his reputation, was at risk. Sourav accepted both the challenges and mitigated the risk accordingly.

Sourav Ganguly was unlike any other Indian captain who had played the game before him. For instance, he belonged to the state of Bengal, an Indian State not known to have produced many great cricketers at the international level both before and after him. In many ways, Sourav's selection in 1992 and later in 1997 had raised a few eyebrows with many hailing the selection as a result of east zone quota. Sourav silenced all his critics with his performance and quickly emerged as the captain of the Indian team. Chants of 'Dada' became common at cricketing grounds and he delighted them with his cricketing intellect and scores. How did he manage to break the barrier and lead the Indian cricket team?

There was always an undeclared system which was created favouring players from a few regions while overlooking those from the rest. Consider for instance, players from Maharashtra, Punjab, Karnataka, Delhi and Tamil Nadu constitute more than 50 per cent of the total number of players who have represented the country. While there is no denying the talent of the players from these states, it is evident that the other Indian states must have players who equally deserved an opportunity to play for the national side. Sourav was a non-conformist in this very onset itself as he belonged to a state not known for cricket before him. In fact, at the time of his debut West Bengal was known to the rest of India for two things—politics and sweets.

Prior to him, only four cricketers from the state, including Sourav, have played 25 or more Test matches for the country. This small list comprises of players such as Dilip Doshi, Pankaj Roy, Sourav himself and the current Indian Test wicketkeeper Wriddhiman Saha. In many ways, he was a trend setter for a state whose first love had been soccer before his arrival in the game.

Since his father was an official with CAB, he could have easily used his influence to warrant the selection of his son. However, if Chandidas Ganguly had to use his influence, would he not have used for his elder son Snehasish Ganguly who was also playing Ranji Trophy. Clearly, Sourav had won his place on the side through his own efforts and skills. His performance had vindicated the same.

Here are some of the challenges and risks that he faced as captain and player.

Negating Regional Favouritism and Team Building

Prior to his arrival, Indian cricket was plagued with regionalism. Normally, in a fourteen-member squad, the last two or three places goes to players depending on the selectors' choices. These choices were largely partisan favouring the players of a particular region to which the selectors belonged. Sourav refused to conform to the norm and put an end to this practice by ensuring that merit becomes the only criteria for selection. There was no longer a lobby for Delhi or Mumbai or Bengaluru, but talented youngsters were getting an opportunity to play for the team. Former India captain Nawab Mansur Ali Khan Pataudi used to say, 'We are not playing for Maharashtra or Delhi or Bengal—we are playing for India'.* But it was Sourav who ensured that the same was brought to practice. It was because of his stand that small-town boys came to the limelight and democratized the process for selection in the Indian squad.

However, his non-conformist stands equally won him several opponents, both in the press as well as within the Board.

Take for instance that a meeting is being convened in your company for the launch of an important product. The CEO, CFO and various product heads voice their opinions in favour of the launch and find nothing wrong with either the product or the launch strategy. Practically, everyone is unanimous about their views that the product will certainly become a great hit in the market. On the contrary, you realize that there is a major flaw that has been overlooked. Will you risk highlighting the same which would make you somewhat of a rebel? If you are someone who always looks at the interests of the company before your own, you will definitely highlight the flaw. Sourav did precisely the same. He believed that it was in the team's interest that such nepotism should not be tolerated.

Building a team is not an easy task, especially when the

---

*https://www.sportskeeda.com/cricket/mak-pataudi-the-man-who-looked-adversity-in-the-eye

sport is followed by hundreds of millions in a cricket-crazy nation. It was the first time that a captain was focussing on building a team that was purely based on talent regardless of the region the players belonged to and at the same time, treating experience with equal respect. It was a stark difference from the regional lobbies that had dominated Indian cricket prior to it. On one hand, Sourav promoted youngsters like Mohd. Kaif, Yuvraj Singh and Zaheer Khan while on the other hand, he equally backed experienced bowlers like Javagal Srinath and Anil Kumble. It was at Sourav's insistence that Javagal Srinath returned from his retirement to lead the bowling attack for World Cup 2003. As captain of the squad, Sourav knew that he needed both the experience of seasoned players as well as the exuberance of the youth.

Building a team is an extremely risky activity. Imagine a group of individuals with different sets of skills hailing from distinct backgrounds, will they be willing to listen to each other? Ego clashes in a corporate setup resulting from differences in opinions and hierarchy is quite common. Sourav had to ensure that there is proper bonding among the players to ensure that results are delivered. He had to make sure that the yardsticks are same for anyone playing in the team.

Ego clashes are quite common in sports. A case in point is when footballer Roy Keane walked out of the Irish Football team in the 2002 FIFA World Cup. Keane alleged that some of the players did not like him and there was a fall-out with the team managers. In a corporate space too, there could be a situation where the star performer might resign in the middle of a critical project, leaving the team in jeopardy.

Mitigating the Risk

Sourav's way of mitigating the risk and ensuring that the team he has built stays together was simple—communication. Ensuring that there was proper communication meant everyone had a voice. For example, in the 2003 Cricket World Cup, India had separate batting, fielding and bowling captains. On one hand, it relieved pressure from Sourav giving him multiple viewpoints to consider, on the other hand, it got the players more involved with the game. Coach John Wright also played a noteworthy role in promoting this 'we' culture than the 'me' culture that existed in the team by maintaining a low-key profile. Another small way was that individual successes were celebrated as the team's success.

When talent meets opportunity, magic happens. It is said that when start-ups are funded by venture capitalists and angel investors, some of the firms go on to become unicorns. (Unicorns are start-up companies which are worth more than a billion dollars such as Paytm or Uber). Sourav followed a careful strategy of mentoring these youngsters with talent and ensuring that Indian cricket is made richer by their contribution. He ensured that each individual knew what his role was in the team and is not over burdened with expectations. For example, Sehwag's responsibility in ODIs was to give a quick-start to the team and not aim at scoring centuries. Occasionally, he would fail in giving the start, but as long as he was contributing to the team's success he would remain a part of the core team.

Youngsters at His Own Risk

In a major change from the selection procedure prior to Sourav, youngsters got a lot of opportunities to perform and cement their place in the team. As captain, he was prepared to risk losing in order to provide a deserving youngster enough opportunities. For example, Sourav's slump in form in ODIs came after he gave up the opening slot to Virender Sehwag.

The Indian cricket team selection committee at that time was plagued with regional bias. Sourav took the stand that the team should be selected purely on merit. He believed that as long as he delivered results, he will be fine taking on the selectors. He wanted to build a team that he believed could win matches. In the 2001 series against Australia, selectors were unwilling to field Harbhajan. Sourav insisted that he won't leave till Harbhajan's name is on that list. Harbhajan Singh later won the Man of the Series award in the same series.

Managing Selectors

This was probably one area where Sourav needed to handle things in a better way. Being a straightforward person, Sourav was quite used to voicing his opinions on matters and challenging the authority of the team's selectors if he felt that they are being unjust. He ensured Anil Kumble's selection during the 2003–04 tour to Australia even when the selectors told him that if India didn't do well, he might lose the captaincy.

However, his dealings with selectors cost him his place amidst the Greg Chappell controversy when national selectors decided to side with the Australian. Could Sourav have handled this situation in a better manner? That's for him to reflect upon. *But in real life,* one of the roles of a successful risk manager is to ensure that the stakeholder's expectations are managed smartly. Probably, Sourav underestimated the impact the issue might have on his career and hence was candid enough to accept when BCCI tried to broker a truce between the captain and the coach. Resolving conflicts is an essential part of risk mitigation.

There are several key lessons to be learnt from this incident for any professional. In order to succeed, we must chalk out a clear plan before reacting to a situation. To be successful in managing risks, we need to look at a planned strategy.

- Accept the risk: The first step is in accepting the risk. Until you accept that a problem exists, there is no way you can come up with a solution. Perhaps, Sourav erred in this very aspect by believing that the team management and board will stand firmly behind him against a foreign coach who was hardly three months with the team. He vastly underestimated the various political motives which was also supporting the decision. For someone who had not even scored 1,500 Test runs—Kiran More had 1,285 runs—to act against Sourav was simply unbelievable. Yet, such events do occur in the corporate life as well—a deserving candidate does not get the promotion and is forced to quit. Sourav's case was largely-weakened as he was not scoring enough runs with his bat while helming the team.
- Avoid the risk: The best way to deal with any risk is by finding alternate solutions. Sourav had a couple of alternatives—he could have spoken with the coach and bought more time by which he might have gotten back into form. One must not forget that he had just scored a century against Zimbabwe after which the controversy erupted.
- Transfer the risk: Another way to handle the situation

could have been that Sourav allowed the BCCI to act on his behalf instead of the matter being discussed in the Press. BCCI at that time was still being led by Jagmohan Dalmiya who was known to favour Sourav. Similarly, in our personal lives too, if we are unable to provide an appropriate response to taking a risk, we should let others manage it for us.
- Mitigate the risk: Sourav could have looked at addressing the issues which was causing the conflict. Not very long ago during the 2003–04 tour, Greg Chappell had guided him in Australia from a personal level and the differences with Greg as coach could have been resolved with proper communication. This is subjected to the fact that both sides are willing to come to a conclusion. It seems unlikely though if in this case this approach would have worked.
- Exploit the risk: Though in this case it was not applicable, considering Sourav felt Greg was the best person to have as coach, yet it is a possible scenario in business. For example, while the advent of a new technology might mean higher capital expenditure, it equally indicates opportunity to improve efficiency.

Breaking the Convention

As Captain, Sourav was quite open to experimenting with the team, several young players made their way into the team. There is an inherent risk associated with it as inexperience might sometimes crumble under pressure. However, Sourav was keen on building the team for the future. It was the junior players he had groomed which formed the core of Dhoni's team when he lifted the World Cup in 2011.

Sourav even experimented with existing players. For example, in his keen interest to have Rahul Dravid in the One-Day team squad, it made Dravid emerge as the wicketkeeper of the side. This in turn provided the much-needed balance to the One-Day team. Experimenting with skills of players is a risky business indeed. However, if they have their leader's faith and support, it can bring out the best in any cricketer. As a matter of fact, Rahul Dravid emerged as the second best Indian wicketkeeper in ODIs after M.S. Dhoni for India with 2,300 runs (4 centuries and 14 fifties) at an average of 44.23.

Years later, Greg Chappell too tried a similar experiment with Irfan Pathan by turning him into a batting all-rounder who could also bowl and field. The experiment gave good results in the beginning with Irfan contributing both with the batting and bowling.

Tryst With Foreign Coach

Till the year 2000, the Indian cricket team has never had a foreign coach. In fact, most coaches prior to that have had stints not more than 1–2 years. If we look at the list of coaches that India have had before 2000, this is how it will read:

Table 5.1
Indian Cricket Team Coaches (1990–2000)

Sl. No.	Coach	Start Year	End Year
1	Bishen Singh Bedi	1990	1991
2	Abbas Ali Baig	1991	1992
3	Ajit Wadekar	1992	1996

4	Sandeep Patil	1996	1996
5	Madan Lal	1996	1997
6	Anshuman Gaekwad	1997	1999
7	Kapil Dev	1999	2000

As all previous coaches were former Indian players, they naturally had a bias towards certain players. It was amidst this that former world cup-winning captain Kapil Dev was appointed as the coach of the Indian team with Sachin Tendulkar as captain of the side. It was a pair made in heaven as both the cricketers were extremely respected by the cricketing fraternity. However, the pair was extremely short-lived as Kapil Dev's name got dragged into the match-fixing controversy and Sachin Tendulkar resigned from the post as it was impacting his game. It was at this juncture that Sourav took over the reign of the team, steered it past the controversy and turned it into a world-class team.

Sourav saw a possibility of building a team here as players were given a fair chance before being dropped. They were selected only on the basis of their performance with no regional bias towards any player. In order to fulfil this dream, Sourav looked at the eventuality of having a foreign coach. A foreign coach would have no intention to indulge in the internal politics of BCCI and will just be concerned with carrying out his responsibilities. Sourav met his rightful match in former New Zealand player John Wright. Together the duo created a partnership that led India to become a formidable team in both conditions—home and overseas. In John Wright's words regarding the partnership he said, 'That was a fantastic time (in Indian cricket). We challenged each other. We had endless debates, there were times when we agreed and disagreed. We all were passionate about working together.'*

In any relation, respect is the very foundation on which a team is built on. Sourav through his decision of having a foreign coach paved the way for future coaches of Team India like Greg Chappell, Duncan Fletcher and Gary Kirsten before the mantle of Indian team's coach returned to the people of the country. However, by that time, several small-town boys had already made their mark in Indian cricket and the dominance of certain regions in the team was on a decline.

Learning Tip

Never shy away from experimenting and trying out new things in order to succeed in your goals.

Evaluation Using Risk Matrix

Risk matrices are widely used during risk assessment to define the level of risk and whether or not it is sufficiently controlled. Each of these is plotted with respect to severity (Y-axis) of the event against the probability of its happening (X-axis). In the modified risk matrix that I have created, the X-axis consists of the phase in Sourav's life plotted against the severity of the risk that he handled.

Sourav has clearly handled several ups and downs in his life. Yet, after each occasion he has been able to bounce back stronger to conquer the situation. If we look at the table above, the two most critical periods in his life was when he was dropped from the team in 1992 and 2005. His life taught us to take

---

*https://sports.ndtv.com/cricket/john-wright-on-sourav-ganguly-we-challenged-each-other-1545859

calculated risks and execute our strategies in a planned manner. His appetite for risk meant that he was always open to change and mould himself according to the situation. This is a lesson that all of us should learn from him.

Figure 5.2
Sourav's Career Evaluation Using Risk Matrix

Extensive				Fall-out with Greg Chappell; loses place in side	
Major	Dropped from team after just 1 match				
Medium		Creating a place in the side and accepting captaincy; match-fixing controversy	Deteoriation in batting form for 2 years	Makes comeback in a do-or-die situation in South Africa and re-establishes himself	IPL controversy; loses his captaincy
Minor	Marries his childhood sweetheart in secret		Encourages youngsters; India emerges as new force	Retirement from international cricket	New role as CAB president and other investments
No impact					
Impact/ Period	Early Life	1997–2000	2000–2005	2005–2008	Beyond 2008

> **Learning Tip**
> Take calculated risks and execute your strategies in a planned manner.

The situation of Sourav is similar to that of an honest member in a corporate setup. He knows his responsibilities, does not mind asking a few rightful questions and does his job in the best interests of the organization. He has also been raising the demand for pay hike for domestic Ranji Trophy players and playing with the pink ball for day-night Test matches. Sourav has been quite vocal that the day-night Test matches are the future of the game if one has to retain the interest in Test cricket.

While Sourav can be labelled as a rebel, he is more of a visionary who is prepared to break the age-old customs to achieve goals. There is a slight difference between the two. We generally merge them in our analysis and understanding. Sourav's non-conformist stand and risk-taking attitude should be looked at in a positive way aimed at improving the existing processes and identifying the gaps plaguing the system. There are few qualities which distinguish him from any other rebel:

- He pushes against an idea while advocating a better alternative
- He believes in the team culture
- He invokes his own authority to push his agenda rather than undermining others' authority

Sometimes how we view a person depends on the vantage point that we look at him from. Perhaps, it is incorrect to look at Sourav as either a rebel or a non-conformist. Instead, Sourav should be looked at as a protagonist in building Team India as we now know it. His decisions and views are a reflection of how he sees the future for the game. Sourav can be seen as a rebel, but there is no leader who can be seen as a leader without having a little rebel inside him or her. We may like him or hate him but we can never ignore his contributions towards the game. He challenges the situation and speaks his mind as long as he sees it in the interest of his team. Whom would you prefer—a leader who is rebel or a rebel who is a leader? If rebels are detrimental to the interests of the team, one must not forget the contributions of leaders like Martin Luther King. Perhaps, we should change the prism through which we look at such leaders.

Grooming Future Leaders

A mentor is someone who sees more talent and ability within you, than you see in yourself, and helps bring it out of you.

—Bob Proctor, American author and motivational speaker

What does mentorship really mean? Is it just providing support to individuals in need and guiding them, or does it include more than this? Mentoring can be looked at as a powerful personal development tool where two persons share knowledge and guidance based on mutual trust and respect. Imagine a new comer in your business team. In a new atmosphere, it is natural that he will begin to feel lost amidst all the chaos and pressure. It is in those situations that a mentor comes handy who shows him the way.

According to a survey in professional social network LinkedIn, almost 70 per cent of India's young workforce lack proper mentorship. They do not know whom to reach out to with respect to handling a crisis or how to plan their career. In sports as well, mentors are equally important. One can easily argue that sports teams have coaches to guide, so why do we need mentors? It is extremely beneficial if the coach of a particular player is also his mentor, but this is generally not the case. Mentorship is an informal relationship and it takes a lot of effort to create a relation based on trust and mutual respect for each other. There is no hierarchy or authority in this relation and it can be among peers as well. It is inherently here that the difference between a coach and a mentor lies. However, great coaches can be good mentors as well. For example, the coach of the Indian cricket captain Virat Kohli, Mr Rajkumar Sharma, also acts as a mentor for him and guides him whenever he makes a mistake. Having a mentor helps in understanding your own strengths in a much better way and ensuring that you are always on track to achieve your goal.

Mentoring in cricket is not new. Australia under Steve Waugh was among the first to adopt mentoring techniques effectively. After retirement, Steve continues to mentor young players all over the world. Sourav Ganguly too belongs to the same mould of leaders. He believed in grooming young talent to ensure that they achieve their full potential in their careers. Furthermore, he launched Vision 2020 for Bengal cricket where he roped in the services of stalwarts like M. Muralitharan, Waqar Younis and V.V.S. Laxman to train young cricketers from the state.

Early Mentorship

Sourav was fortunate to be born into a wealthy family with several associations with the cricketing world. In the words of his brother Snehasish, their father was instrumental in ensuring that both the brothers got the right infrastructure to practise the game.

Our father built a multi-gym in our house. We had concrete wickets with nets at home by 1987. Sourav and I always got a lot of help from my father. He pushed us, and both of us were fanatics too. We trained together for six–seven years. We have always been close. Once I finished playing, I always spoke to him about his game. I tried to help him as much as I could. He took my advice seriously and I'd like to think I helped him.*

Sourav had the benefit of two mentors who were willing to help and guide him at all times without any vested interests. Snehasish too was a cricketer (first class career from 1986/87 to 1996/97) and his guidance helped Sourav a lot in improving his own game. As both the brothers were playing together in Ranji and domestic cricket, they enjoyed each other's company and were willing to exchange suggestions and advices. It was the same kind of relationship that Sourav later built with the young players in the Indian dressing room who fondly called him 'Dada' (elder brother).

In the 1989–90 season of Ranji Trophy, Snehasish played in all the matches throughout the season but was dropped in the finals and Sourav was selected instead of him. On the day of his selection, Sourav tried to avoid Snehasish as if he had done something wrong. However, after Snehahish had spoken to him, things became normal again. In his brother, Sourav had found someone who will always stand by his side and guide him in the years to come.

The story of Snehasish being dropped is very similar to Mark Waugh being selected instead of Steve Waugh when he

---

*https://www.wisdenindia.com/cricket-article/snehasish-ganguly-story-bravery-broken-leg/158772

made his debut in Test cricket. In circumstances such as these it is common for a sibling rivalry to emerge. However, Snehasish's maturity meant that Sourav understood the true essence and quality that a mentor should possess. It was later with the same unselfish attitude that Sourav mentored and fought for young players in the Indian team.

Sourav, however, looked at his father as his mentor. He had an extremely significant influence on Sourav and his brother's cricketing careers as they were put under the guidance of current Saurashtra coach Debu Mitra. Later, Sourav went to play in English conditions under the guidance of Mr Mitra. In an interview in 1996, Sourav was candid enough to acknowledge the influence his father had in his cricketing career. When asked who had the biggest influence on him, Sourav was quick to respond that it was 'My father. He is very keen on cricket and would sacrifice anything to enable us play cricket. He wanted me to be a cricketer and I am happy that I did not let him down.'*

The father-son relationship had also transformed into a mentor-mentee relationship in this case. Any individual who has received proper guidance from early childhood will understand the meaning and purpose of discipline in their lives. Teachers play a similar role in shaping us from our school days.

Learning Tip

It is extremely beneficial if you find a mentor at a very early stage in your career.

---

*http://www.sportstarlive.com/cricket/indian/teammates-supported-me/article8751983.ece

Mentee Turns Mentor

During his period as captain of Team India, more number of young players were selected and given a fair number of opportunities as part of the squad. The one aspect that probably distinguished Sourav from other captains in the past was his ability and intent to support the players. Whenever a player went through a poor form, Sourav would fight for the player in front of the selector. The ability to build an entire team from scratch is what makes a great captain. Much like Imran Khan and Arjuna Ranatunga, Sourav's contribution in this regard is unmatched. It was his perseverance and guidance for the individuals that yielded several star performers for the country.

Some of the cricketers he mentored are:

- **Yuvraj Singh:** The stylish left-handed batsman emerged as one the most attacking players in ODI and T20 cricket. He was also the Player of the Tournament in both ICC T20 World Cup 2007 and ICC ODI World Cup 2011. His stint with cancer (from which he successfully recovered) impacted his performance and kept him away from the game for some time. His last game was against West Indies in June 2017. He is one among five Indians to have achieved the feat of playing 300 One-Day games.

    Yuvraj was also a fine all-rounder and his ability to take wickets at critical junctures was instrumental in ensuring India's success.

    The cricketer has often spoken about Sourav being the best captain that he has played under, while Sourav maintained and kept faith in his abilities at all times. In an interview in September 2017, Sourav maintained that Yuvraj can still make a comeback to the national side. It is this mutual respect that has built the foundation of this relationship.

- **Zaheer Khan**

  Sourav's abilities to spot talent and back such cricketers was a significant part of his career. Zaheer Khan was one such find who spearheaded India's bowling attack for a long time. In his illustrious career, Zaheer played 200 ODI internationals, 92 Test matches and 17 T20s taking over 600 international wickets.

  Yet again Sourav was quick to spot talent when he first saw Zaheer in action in Nairobi during the 2000 ICC Knockout Trophy. In his own words, '…when I saw him in Nairobi, I thanked the almighty: Maybe, my dream of making India a good team overseas will materialize.'* The Indian team had always lacked a quality left-arm pacer and Zaheer Khan filled the void. It was Sourav's ability to back these youngsters that has today transformed India into a formidable side.

- **Mohammad Kaif**

  He came into the Indian side after winning the U-19 World Cup as captain. The stylish right-handed batsman was known for his ability to score quick singles. His knock of 87 in the Natwest Trophy final is remembered even today, along with his partnership with Yuvraj Singh which ensured a nearly impossible win for India. Unfortunately, his career ended prematurely due to lack of consistency with the bat and increased competition in the middle-order. His last international match was against South Africa in 2006.

---

*https://www.sportskeeda.com/cricket/sourav-ganguly-speaks-about-retired-legends-virender-sehwag-zaheer-khan

- **Harbhajan Singh**
  Arguably, Sourav's greatest find, Harbhajan Singh, emerged as one of the finest off-spinners in the modern version of the game. His early career was mired in chucking controversy. However, Sourav picked him up for the 2001 Australia series, where Harbhajan decimated the Australian batting earning himself the nickname, 'Turbanator'. Apart from over 700 international wickets, Harbhajan also has scored over 3,500 international runs.

  During the Sourav–Greg Chappell controversy, Harbhajan was among the few cricketers who spoke openly in support of Sourav and accused Chappell of instilling fear and insecurity among the players. Here was a mentee who was standing in support of his mentor when it mattered the most; clearly it spoke volumes of the role Sourav must have played in his career. Harbhajan went on to say that Sourav is an excellent captain and rubbished all of Chappell's claims.
- **Virender Sehwag**
  Virender Sehwag a.k.a. 'Viru' was one of the most attacking openers that India has ever produced. He is the only Indian with two triple centuries in Test matches. Sehwag had an extremely illustrious career where he instilled fear in the minds of the bowler. However, when it was difficult to find a place for Virender in the Test team, Sourav promoted him as an opener as he did not wish to miss out on this talent. In the One-Day team, Sourav gave up his place as the opener, breaking an extremely successful opening partnership with Sachin in favour of Sehwag. Providing the right platform and sacrifices like these helped Sehwag emerge as the destructive batsman we knew of.

  Sehwag acknowledged Sourav's sacrifice and even hailed

him partially responsible for the rise of M.S. Dhoni. He said, 'Ganguly at that time decided to give Dhoni a chance at No.3 for three or four matches. There are very few captains who would first give away his own batting spot for Virender Sehwag and then his set spot of No.3 for Dhoni.'*

The two shared a bit of banter over twitter during the selection of a coach for Team India. However, they were quick to resolve the same. Their relationship is based on trust more than anything else.

- **Ashish Nehra**

The lanky speedster from Delhi was another of Sourav's finds. In an injury-prone career lasting for nearly two decades, Nehra spearheaded the attack with his control of the swinging ball. He is best remembered for his performance against England in the 2003 World Cup. After an extremely long career, he recently retired from international cricket in 2017.

The way Sourav developed and built his team was remarkable. They enjoyed a bonhomie like a family and even pranked each other. On one instance on 1 April, Yuvraj Singh created a few fake newspaper articles with comments attributed to Sourav Ganguly that he had negatively spoken about the other players in the team. While Sourav denied making such comments, players like Harbhajan and Zaheer too acted in support. A teary-eyed Sourav even offered to resign, it was then that Rahul Dravid spoke the truth that it was just a prank on April Fool's day. An angry Sourav

---

*https://www.indiatvnews.com/sports/cricket-exclusive-virender-sehwag-reveals-sourav-ganguly-s-sacrifice-behind-ms-dhoni-s-success-405230

Ganguly chased Yuvraj Singh and the others out of the dressing room with his bat. It was a team well built. A light-hearted mentor can sometimes enjoy the prank of his protégés.

In a public event, Sourav was candid to admit the influence Imran Khan had on him during the period when he was removed from captaincy and dropped from the team. In his own words:

It was tough, but it made me a better person. I once met Imran Khan in Lahore during that period. He was actually following Indian cricket. We have a fantastic relationship, Imran and myself. He said something to me which I always remember in life. When you fly high and see dark clouds, you find a way to fly higher. I remembered those words during that (tough) period.*

It is significant to note that such encouraging words and support is required by everyone including someone as strong as Sourav. It definitely helps when someone you respect shows their faith in your ability.

Learning Tip
Look up to advice from others at all points in your career.

---

*https://www.hindustantimes.com/cricket/sourav-ganguly-reveals-how-imran-khan-came-to-his-aid-during-greg-chappell-era/story-iE5JhDe9hLc4oiy6AGflUO.html

His Support for His Ranji Team

Sourav started his career in Ranji cricket in the 1989–90 season when Bengal won the trophy. After three years of Ranji cricket, he finally got a break into the Team India but only for a single match. However, it was short-lived as he went onto become a regular member of the Indian team 1997 onwards. In that period, Sourav rarely played for the Bengal side. His real test with the Ranji team came in 2005 when he was dropped from the national side. Sourav gave up the captaincy of the Bengal team as well and wanted his deputy Deep Dasgupta to lead. In that moment of crisis, instead of thinking about his own career, Sourav believed that it was time for Deep to fill in the shoes of the skipper and lead the side. He wanted the youngsters to face the challenges themselves so that they are prepared for the future.

In times of crisis, the true character of a person can be judged. There are very few cricketers who could have done the same. It was an opportunity for Sourav to lead his team to victory so that the selectors take notice. Yet, he once again proved his selflessness when it mattered. If you consider Sourav's tenure as the India skipper, very few players from the state actually got a chance to play for the team. There is an important lesson to be learnt from this—his decisions were purely driven by merit.

It is quite common in the corporate life to encounter a manager who supports only people from his region or with a background similar to his own. It happens as we tend to find similarities and hence a natural preference for the other develops. While this may sound good on paper, such decisions cannot be the basis of a great team. A team should be based only on merit and selected purely on performance. Even though, Sourav mentored the Bengal players, he did not influence their selection as he felt there were other better players around.

Learning Tip
Always choose a team which is based on merit and not on personal preference.

In 2017, Sourav even mentored the Bengal team before the semi-final of the Vijay Hazare Cup, where Bengal took on Jharkhand. The Jharkhand team was being led by M.S. Dhoni and hence Sourav's inputs were needed for the young Bengal team led by Manoj Tiwari. It is noteworthy to remember that a lot of these players looked up to Sourav as their role model. His advices gave huge dividends as Bengal was able to defeat Jharkhand by 41 runs in the semi-finals. The experience that Sourav brings to the table is no less than that of a sharp-thinking CEO. It is his ability to plan ahead and bring to the fore all of his previous experiences that makes him an extremely formidable opponent in the cricketing field.

Mentorship breeds loyalty. It is not dependent on the age or relation between two persons. A clear incident that shows the influence of Sourav on the Bengal cricketers can be drawn from an incident that took place in 2015 during a Ranji game between Delhi and Bengal. Gautam Gambhir had spoken against Sourav Ganguly which did not go down well with Manoj Tiwary and the two had a heated argument. Why did he need to pick up a fight for Sourav? When someone guides you without any motive, it builds a strong gratitude for the person. When in office, if your boss also acts as your mentor, will you ever leave that team? Probably never.

Mentoring IPL Teams

As a part of IPL teams, Sourav was instrumental in mentoring several young players of KKR such as Ashok Dinda and Wriddhiman Saha. Like a professor who was examining the students, Sourav would often suggest smaller things to these young players. It is always the 2 per cent extra effort that produces the result and creates the difference between winning and losing. Even when Sourav was not picked for the KKR squad in later years, its co-owner Juhi Chawla was extremely keen on having Sourav as a mentor. There can be no denying the fact that Sourav had one of the sharpest cricketing minds and his interest in guiding others was admired by many. In his last stint in the IPL, Sourav acted as the mentor and captain of the Pune IPL team. Its owner, Subrata Roy of Sahara Group, felt that Sourav with his vast experience can significantly contribute to the team's success.

If we consider Sourav's eagerness to mentor individuals, we find that he tends to give back to the youngsters and help in their development. This is an important quality to have as a mentor. There can be individuals who might be exceptional at their work, but when it comes to guiding youngsters, they might fail miserably. Equally, the reverse might also be true as someone who has seen lot of failures may turn out to be an excellent mentor. In case of Sourav, he combines both these worlds—he has seen the highs and lows, the joy of leading the team to being dropped unceremoniously—there can perhaps be no better mentor than him.

If we try to plot Sourav's abilities, they seem to fit perfectly to be an ideal mentor.

Figure 6.1
Sourav Ganguly Attributes as Mentor

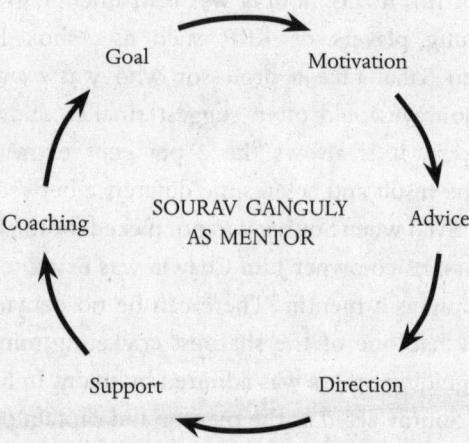

In each of the areas, Sourav has proven to be an excellent mentor. If we try to decode one of the major reasons for his success, it has also been his approachability. He is not at all hesitant to reach out to others if he needs support and is equally accessible when others need him. His humility and simple lifestyle further adds credence to this fact. In his current role as the president of CAB, he realized that young cricketers from the state needed a good bowling mentor and did not hesitate to reach out to former Pakistani great Waqar Younis for help. As a mentor and an individual if he feels that a particular decision will help the larger interests of the team, he is not the kind to take a step back.

Learning Tip
Being humble and approachable is the
first step to become a successful mentor.

Coaching the Kids

Sourav Ganguly has also launched the Sourav Ganguly Foundation and Cricket School which aims to collaborate with other schools to promote sports at the grassroot level. The school aims to provide free coaching to those cricketers who are not financially strong but talented. He says, 'We will make sure that we sit with the schools and create a curriculum which is not just about studies, but also involves a considerable amount of sport'.* In a country like India where education often takes precedence over sports, this is a welcome move taken by one of the sports icons of the country. Perhaps, this is his way of giving back to the society.

There are several advantages for anyone who seeks to be a mentor. While coaches and trainers help in knowing where you are in your career and developing specific skill set, a mentor helps in facilitating your all-round development. It is similar to Sourav stepping down as captain of the Bengal team to develop Deep Dasgupta's leadership skills. It is not necessary for a mentor hailing from the same industry as yours; it is important that the person has encountered similar experiences. This will enable the mentor to successfully understand the situation and guide his mentees. Being a mentor has significant advantages as it helps in enriching your life in the following ways:

- **Building communication skills:** Your teammate or office colleague may not belong to the same region as you do or have the same background. Mentoring such an individual will definitely broaden your horizon and

---

*https://www.indiatoday.in/sports/cricket/story/sourav-ganguly-foundation-and-cricket-school-launched-357568-2016-12-14

improve your skills.
- **Encountering new perspectives:** Working with someone young and new will enable you to gain a fresh perspective on a plethora of things. He or she will have new perspectives and views which will enable you to enrich your own skill set.
- **Career advancement:** In today's world, ability to show that you have helped advance others' career also acts as criterion when it comes to professional growth in a company.
- **Build your own leadership skills:** Guiding someone new will also help in building your own leadership skills as he or she will come up with new questions and challenges for you to encounter. It will help you in enhancing your leadership skills.
- **Self-satisfaction:** It definitely creates a feel-good factor when you are able to guide someone and help in resolving their queries.

In today's world, attrition is an important issue faced by all companies. Young employees need to be motivated and guided by their seniors. In such a scenario, it is important that companies should look at having a mentorship program within the firm. This will help in judging the employee satisfaction level as well as ensuring a right role suitable for the employees. Some of the top companies such as Google and General Electric that have included a mentorship program have been enormously successful in retaining their key talent. Just like it helped Sourav build the core for his Team India, it can equally help any company in building its right team.

Learning Tip

Having a formal mentorship program in an organization can help in retaining the right talent for the firm.

Power of Aggression

There is a difference between being a leader and being a boss. Both are based on authority. A boss demands blind obedience; a leader earns his authority through understanding and trust.

—Klaus Balkenhol, German equestrian
and Olympic gold medallist

Aggression can be seen as the act of quickly achieving objectives using force or conduct. If we look at the definition given by authors Robert A. Baron and Deborah R. Richardson, it says, 'any form of behaviour directed towards the goal of harming of injuring another live being who is motivated to avoid such treatment.' By the very onset of the definition, aggression is often characterized by a negative connotation. Yet, nothing can be further than the truth. Aggressive leaders have often produced great results in sports, business and battlefields. It is generally mental aggression that takes precedence over physical aggression. It is quite often that in corporate life we encounter individuals who are extremely hostile and pushy in nature. Imagine that your boss at work exhibits a similar behaviour, will you be receptive towards such an attitude? Quite naturally one will prefer a more friendly behaviour. Now, if I say that it is a sales discussion and the persons who will thrive will be the ones to have the right mix of aggression and the go-getter attitude.

In sports too, things are not very different. The game of rugby, for instance, is dependent on the aggression of the player to ensure that he reaches the goal. Soccer too is seen in a similar context with the skill mixed with aggression in more successful players. Sport is perhaps a perfect simulation of a business war room. Unlike physical play, business discussions are led with numbers coupled with aggressive targets.

It is equally important to showcase controlled aggression. Sometimes uncontrolled aggression can cost the team a well-deserved victory. In the 2006 FIFA World Cup final, French captain Zinedine Zidane was provoked by Italian defender Marco Materazzi through his remarks about his family. Zidane responded with an infamous head butt which earned him a red card and probably cost France the cup. Aggression in sports and business can be focussed towards the goal if three objectives are fulfilled:

The reason for aggression: As any individual, each time we feel charged up we need to ask ourselves this question. Suppose, you have been denied a rightful promotion. The aggression in such a case is often misdirected and might result in inflicting more damage than good. On the other hand, if the aggression is driven by a goal and vision, the situation would be completely different. Here, aggression will be driven towards achieving results by channelizing the energy towards the goal. It will serve as a driving force for arriving at the desired outcome.

Control: Aggression which is controlled can lead to success for an individual in any sphere of life. It is significant to look at the difference between appearing strong and appearing aggressive. So one should exercise control in terms of the body language that we adopt towards our team members and opponents. Our body language should reflect control and not authority—the very difference why leaders motivate people while often loathe tasks given by bosses.

Tone: The tone in which we express our aggression should reflect our goal without any kind of personal motive towards achieving the purpose.

Cricket, unlike soccer and rugby, has largely been considered a gentleman's game. It has been regarded as a sport dependent largely on skills and not on physical aggression. Still, a positive mental aggression begins to play a more relevant role even in the cricket. It is said that a game is won in the mind. There is no wonder then that in such a sport, sledging and verbal assault are used by the world-dominating Australian side to decimate the opposing team even before the match begins.

Sourav was arguably the first Indian captain who decided to respond to the Aussies in their own game with his aggression on and off the field. The incident started when Steve Waugh was forced to wait for the toss in the 2001 India-Australia series in Vizag. The incident started the India-Australia rivalry of modern era as during the series India stopped the historic 16-match victory march of the Aussie team. Sourav later revealed that the incident was a result of retaliation over an incident involving Aussie coach John Buchanan and Javagal Srinath. He said during an interview that:

> It was not his (Buchanan's) business. Srinath told us in a team meeting that Buchanan had asked him that (why he was leaving the field) in a rude manner. Then we decided that we would show them... That's why I went out late for the toss in Vizag (third ODI in April).*

Even during this incident, Sourav showed his stature in expressing a very controlled aggression-aided response to the situation. Yet, he was careful in presenting the same to the media at that time by diverting the attention in a subtle manner, 'There's so much to do in the mornings, knocking up, talking to the selectors, that I may have been late by a few minutes.'**

It is interesting to note that by saying so Sourav not only served his purpose of giving the Aussies a response but also was clever enough to avoid any action from the match referee. The strategy seemed to work as India managed to get the better of the Australian team for most part of the hard-fought series. While Australians play aggressive cricket, they are also among the first to appreciate when the opponent plays well. The strategy seemed to have worked at that time as Steve Waugh later conceded in his autobiography *Out of My Comfort Zone* that the incident had wounded him up. Aggression need not be associated with strong words but can sometimes be subtle in nature.

If you have a meeting setup with a vendor where you wish to drive a hard bargain on the price, it is very rare that the meeting will start on time. The reason is that by being late for

---

*https://www.hindustantimes.com/india/i-was-deliberately-late-for-toss-ganguly/story-x6eesSB7ax0cNNMHvUlB4J.html
**https://www.hindustantimes.com/india/i-was-deliberately-late-for-toss-ganguly/story-x6eesSB7ax0cNNMHvUlB4J.html

a short while, each side tries to drive a point that the deal is not significant enough to impact profits immensely for the party. This is done in order to reduce the room for negotiation and ensure the prices stay fixed. Sourav tried to do exactly the same. He wanted to set the ground rule that though the Australians may be world champions, they are playing a new Indian team on their own turf. He wanted to shatter the Aussie mindset of winning by rattling the Indian team using mind games.

Learning tip

It is important to set agenda using subtle forms of aggression to achieve the desired outcome.

If we try to plot these three approaches using the same incident, this is how Sourav's aggression will look like:

Figure 7.1
Sourav's Aggression: Objective, Control and Tone

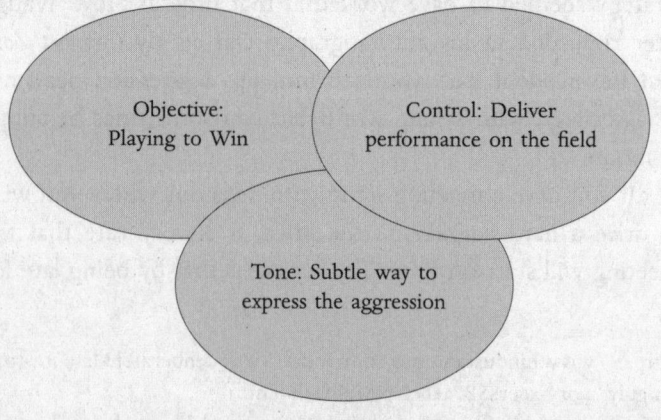

It is important here to note that Sourav used his aggression to further his goal of winning the game. In the follow-up tour of India to Australia in 2003–04, Steve Waugh asked Sourav if he would be late for the toss again. Sourav responded in kind by saying if the Aussies behaved well, he wouldn't. Quite a witty reply! He further proved his point by scoring 144 in a pacer-friendly track in Brisbane during the 2003–04 tour. Sourav with his aggression also won the respect of the former Aussie captain as he wrote in his autobiography:

> I saw in Sourav a committed individual who wanted to inject some toughness and combativeness into a side that had often tended in the past to roll over and expose a soft underbelly.*

It is significant to note that Steve acknowledged the fact that Sourav's aggressiveness brought about a change in the mindset and approach of the Indian team to play cricket. Sourav led a team which had two set of players—time and tested senior cricketers like Sachin Tendulkar, Rahul Dravid and Anil Kumble and a fresh bunch of young cricketers like Yuvraj Singh, Harbhajan Singh, Zaheer Khan among others. His aggression played an important role in making the team believe that they can win matches overseas. The Indian team have always been regarded as a formidable team in home conditions; however, they have often struggled in overseas conditions. Sourav was one such captain who brought about this change in Indian cricket. He remains to be the most successful Test captain with 11 overseas wins.

---

*http://www.rediff.com/cricket/2005/dec/01waugh.htm

Table 7.1
Sourav's Overseas Test Wins as Captain
(overseas match wins highlighted)

Year	Opposition	Venue	Matches	Won	Lost	Draw
2000/1	Bangladesh	Bangladesh	1	1	0	0
2000/1	Zimbabwe	India	2	1	0	1
2000/1	Australia	India	3	2	1	0
2001	Zimbabwe	Zimbabwe	2	1	1	0
2001	Sri Lanka	Sri Lanka	3	1	2	0
2001/2	South Africa	South Africa	2	0	1	1
2001/2	England	India	3	1	0	2
2001/2	Zimbabwe	India	2	2	0	0
2001/2	West Indies	West Indies	5	1	2	2
2002	England	England	4	1	1	2
2002/3	West Indies	India	3	2	0	1
2002/3	New Zealand	New Zealand	2	0	2	0
2003/4	New Zealand	India	1	0	0	1
2003/4	Australia	Australia	4	1	1	2
2003/4	Pakistan	Pakistan	1	1	0	0
2004/5	Australia	India	2	0	1	1
2004/5	South Africa	India	2	1	0	1
2004/5	Bangladesh	Bangladesh	2	2	0	0
2004/5	Pakistan	India	3	1	1	1
2005/6	Zimbabwe	Zimbabwe	2	2	0	0
Total			49	21	13	15

Among his contemporary cricketers, Ricky Ponting came close to being as aggressive as Sourav. If we compare the record of the two players, one can easily see that Ponting is ahead by a distance. However, Sourav did not initially have the kind of team that Ponting commanded. As they say, that a captain is only as good as his team.

If we look at the aggressive approach followed by Virat Kohli, it has been made possible due to the change in the dressing room environment during Sourav's tenure. Former Indian spinner Bishen Singh Bedi recently acknowledged the same by saying the following:

> Sourav Ganguly is one of the finest Indian captains we have had and he was also responsible, in many ways, for the culture that prevails today.*

The major difference between Sourav and Ponting's record was owing to the lack of quality pace bowling attack for India. This resulted in fewer victories in pacer-friendly surfaces overseas. Ponting had a fantastic team with very few weaknesses, an aggressive opening pair of Gilchrist and Hayden, quality fielding side and a bowling line-up that the world was in envy of. Sourav, on the other hand, had an elegant and a world-class team of batsmen at his disposal but lacked the bowling fire power. In recent times though, Indian team has vastly made amends on this front with a pace battery comprising of the likes of Jaspreet Bumrah, Mohd. Shami, Bhuvneshwar Kumar, Ishant Sharma and Umesh Yadav which should give captain Virat Kohli more victories in the years to come.

The reason Sourav's aggressiveness was innate and not owing to circumstances was partly due to his upbringing. Being born in a wealthy family, Sourav never needed to play the game as a career option which led him to play it fearlessly. His first love being soccer also enabled him to develop the aggressive

---

*http://www.dailypioneer.com/sports-bytes/ganguly-responsible-for-current-aggressive-culture-of-indian-team-bedi.html

attitude needed to succeed in the game. In short, Sourav was never worried about taking risks in order to win and succeed in every situation.

A case in point was during the team selection of the Australian tour of 2003–04. The selectors had decided to drop Anil Kumble from the team considering his poor form, but Sourav insisted that he should be a part of the team. Even the then coach John Wright suggested that maybe he should let it go and they should try to do their best with the given team. However, persistent captain Sourav was not willing to give up. He had played long enough with him to know the importance of Kumble for the side and was willing to risk it all. The selectors told him that if Anil is selected and the team does not do well, Sourav would be the first to go. Sourav accepted the challenge. Anil Kumble reposed the faith in his captain and emerged has the most successful bowler that year with 80 Test wickets. In the very same series, Kumble emerged with 24 wickets and was instrumental in ensuring that India retained the Border–Gavaskar trophy. If Sourav wasn't aggressive enough, do you think that Anil Kumble would have got another chance to play for the country? While we may never know the answer to the question, there is little doubt that India would have lost a quality spinner. Just like the incident involving Buchanan and Srinath, here too Sourav stood up for his teammate. His attitude and aggression helped in gaining the faith of his teammates and they put in their best for their leader. Imagine a simple incident: Your office is downsizing and company is planning to lay you off. However, your boss takes a tough stand and ensures that you are given significant time to prove your worth in the changed scenario. Will you ever leave the guidance of such a boss?

Learning Tip

Use your aggression for a desired purpose keeping the interests of the team. This helps in gaining trust and loyalty among the teammates.

Sourav's aggression is backed by two key components: Self-belief and performance. During his career as a captain and player, he realized that absence of either will be counter-productive to his aggression. It will be similar to a false threat; people may treat it seriously once or twice but will eventually ignore the same.

Self-belief + Performance = Desired Outcome

Sourav's aggressive behaviour started paying rich dividends with India beginning to play competitive cricket overseas. Few can forget that Andrew Flintoff took off his shirt in the 2002 series during England's tour of India. The incident took place at the Wankhede Stadium in the ODI which England won. The series was eventually tied at 3-3. Years later, Flintoff regretted the incident by saying that it was embarrassing and was ten seconds of madness. While the entire cricketing fraternity was aghast at the incident, it was particularly humiliating for the Indian team considering a player of their former colonial ruler was now mocking them in their own country. To make matters worse, several British tabloids such as *The Guardian** hailed it as a symbol of a combatant British side in the years to come. One person though was watching the incident as a keen observer and was keen to give a fitting response to the incident, but at an appropriate time.

That opportunity came sooner than expected when India

---
*https://www.theguardian.com/sport/2002/feb/04/cricket.englandinindia200102

won the Natwest Trophy final. India chased a total of 325 to defeat England at the Lord's. Sourav's response was a fitting reply to Andrew Flintoff's action few months earlier as he took off his t-shirt from the Lord's balcony and whirled it around. The world was there to witness that if one approaches this Indian team negatively, it was certain to get a response. The same media which praised Flintoff's action was now aghast and questioned Sourav's behaviour calling it disrespectful for the game.

Such tit-for-tat responses are not uncommon in the corporate world either. Few can forget the ambush marketing launched by Pepsi with its 'Nothing Official about It' campaign when Coca Cola was the official drinking partner of the 1996 Cricket World Cup. It is a normal human tendency to retaliate in case there is an unwarranted aggression; can sports be any different? Soccer is a good example where players routinely get physical during the course of the game. However, once the game is over, the animosity is left behind them.

Sourav's action was largely symbolic. It was meant to be a declaration that his young side was ready to win matches under any situation or condition and playing to win. It was meant to show that this Indian team was no longer afraid to express themselves and respond according to the situation. The transformation journey of the Indian team that he started in 1999 was beginning to bear fruit and eventually leading the team to the 2003 World Cup final.

His aggression can also be reflected into his statement to the press during the 2003–04 Australian tour. Sourav candidly remarked that it will be known how good the side is only after the series. It was a bold statement considering the fact that Indians were known to be susceptible to fast bowling on bouncy tracks and Sourav's own weakness against the short pitched delivery. The series ended tied at 1-1. However, it was clear that Australia's hegemony was under threat by the rising Indian team. It is important to note why Sourav would make such a statement. It was just part of his response in order to ensure that Australians do not get the edge in the mental game.

The real game of sports and business is played in the mind. Every scenario in business, war or sports can be chalked out in a chess board where you have to anticipate the opponent's next move. In such a scenario, it is important to get the first advantage. Sourav did exactly that. In a similar manner when a competitor launches a product in the market, it is common for the market leader to completely ignore the threat in press by saying that their products are superior. In the backend though, the leader is reverse engineering his opponent's products and trying to improve his products in order to stay relevant in the race. When Mukesh Ambani launched Jio, he proclaimed that whatever rates his competitors would offer, Jio will always be cheaper.* It was a clear-cut strategy to destroy the confidence of other players to compete with his venture in a price-sensitive market like India.

Learning Tip
Analyse your opponents carefully and use
your aggression for delivering results
by playing the mental game.

---

*https://www.hindustantimes.com/business-news/mukesh-ambani-promises-cheaper-data-rates-with-reliance-jio-launches-prime-membership/story-5QrIdJn0BzwJhDEFhmWHfJ.html

Avoiding Negative Aggression

The question that comes to everyone's mind is that aggression can also be detrimental to the team's interests by generating conflicts. This situation is not uncommon. If we consider the case of Apple, Steve Jobs had hired John Scully to become the CEO of the company he had founded. John, however, was more driven by balance sheet and profitability and eventually ended up aiding in the firing of Steve Jobs. It was more a case of the clash of two personalities at play here—both aggressive and looking to run things in their own way. It is quite possible that during the course of work we tend to build a little friction between our colleagues. In such a situation, it is imperative that we look at ways in which we can control and channelize our aggression towards the desired goal.

A similar conflict can be looked at the Greg Chappell and Sourav Ganguly controversy. Sourav was instrumental in ensuring the selection of Greg as coach of the Indian team after the departure of John Wright due to personal reasons. Sourav himself felt benefitted with Chappell's guidance during the 2003 tour. However, after assuming the position of coach, relations between the two began to sour. To make matters worse after scoring the century against Zimbabwe, Sourav revealed on television that he had been asked to step down as captain before the match.* While this had made him more determined to perform well, it set the cat loose among the pigeons. This was followed by Chappell's leaked email to BCCI where he lambasted Sourav with all kinds of malicious allegations eventually dividing fans into two groups—those who loved him and those who

---

*http://www.espncricinfo.com/zimvind/content/story/219375.html

wanted him out. Sourav was removed from the team and had to stay out for a period of 10 months from the national side. The incident has even become a case study in Indian B-schools.*

Was television the right mode of expressing the happenings in the dressing room? Perhaps not. It was an action that Sourav could have easily avoided as it brought more harm to his career. Perhaps, if the situation was not made public, there would have been enough room for both Sourav and Greg to reconcile their differences. However, putting this out in the media meant things would never be the same again. The drama that followed ensured one of the most successful captains of the modern game was unfortunately humiliated, removed from captaincy and was kept out of the team for largely non-cricketing reasons.

Learning Tip

Sometimes being aggressive may be counter-productive, so you should show restraint and react according to the situation.

In resolving conflicts such as these, the DISC framework often comes handy. It stands for the various styles of an individual: Dominance, Influence, Steadiness and Conscientiousness. The framework prescribes that depending on the style of the individual, the approach would have to be different. The DISC theory was originally created by psychologist William Marston, whereas the tool was created by Walter Clarke. In case of Sourav and Greg Chappell, both have been captains of their respective teams and wanted to dominate the proceedings. Since

---

*https://www.hindustantimes.com/india/greg-sourav-row-now-a-case-study/story-kb4ZMibkAD0zCCD2UKHfSM.html

dominance-styled individuals are more task-oriented rather than people-oriented, fallout between the two former captains was natural. Another force that worked against Sourav was that he did not take into confidence other senior players during the selection of the coach.* If we compare the captaincy record in Tests of the two personalities, they are extremely similar with Sourav having captained just one additional Test.

Table 7.2
Test Captaincy Record Comparison of
Greg Chappell and Sourav Ganguly

	Period	Matches	Won	Lost	Drawn	Win%
Greg Chappell	1975–83	48	21	13	14	43.75
Sourav Ganguly	2000–06	49	21	13	15	42.86

While several cricket pundits of the time questioned Sourav's attitude and commitment to the game, the reason for the fallout was a clash of two personalities along with petty board politics. Apparently, Greg was given the impression that till Sourav is the captain, he will not have a free hand in taking decisions. To make matters worse, Greg's tenure as coach began when Sourav was serving the 6-match ODI ban and by the time he returned to the team, things had already turned sour. If attitude and commitment was the issue, Sourav would have faced a similar response from other coaches as well during his playing career. Actually, it is quite ironical to even think that if a player is not committed to the game, can he play for over ten years of international cricket?

It is important to compare the reasons behind this conflict using the DISC framework. Let us first look at Sourav with

---

*http://www.espncricinfo.com/ci/content/story/143872.html

John Wright and Greg Chappell using it:

Table 7.3
DISC Framework Analysis of Sourav Ganguly, John Wright and Greg Chappell

	Sourav Ganguly	John Wright	Greg Chappell
Personality	Dominance (largely & Influencing	Influencing	Dominance
Conflict Resolution Technique Preferred	Direct approach	Conversational	Direct approach
Task Oriented/ People Oriented	Task oriented	People oriented	Task oriented
Decision Making	Solution oriented with focus on building relationship	Focus on keeping a positive environment	Solution approach using a direct to the point approach

It was clearly a situation that even individuals can encounter in workplace. Personality differences are not uncommon in any team and it is imperative that we should deal with the situation accordingly. Imagine a boss who consistently complains to you about your attitude and commitment to work. There can be two ways to approach the same:

1. Find a new job
2. Resolve the issues through discussion

Instead, in the above situation, both the parties decided to talk to the media instead of talking among themselves. Both Greg Chappell and Sourav should have acted contrary to their style and avoided a much-hyped drama. BCCI tried to broker peace between the coach and the captain, however it did not result in much. The recent coach-captain controversy involving Virat Kohli and Anil Kumble is also a reminiscent of the earlier incident.

In a corporate setting, who will you rather have as a boss? Sourav faced a similar clash with coach John Buchanan during his IPL stint with Kolkata Knight Riders. There could be two reasons for this clash: 1. Buchanan believed in him being the power and decision centre, or 2. His past experience with Sourav when he was the coach of Australia. Sourav had got under the skin of the Australian team as captain and perhaps it was his way of getting back at him.

Sourav's aggression was not limited to the coaches alone. He was equally vocal on the field. During the final of ICC Champions Trophy in 2002 against Sri Lanka, Russel Arnold was trying to steal a quick run by dabbing the ball on the offside but had to return to the crease. In his bid to return, Arnold had run over the pitch and was quickly pointed out by Sourav. What followed was a verbal argument with the two and Sourav was not the one to back out. Another similar incident happened during the 2007 series against England, when Sourav tore into English bowler Stuart Broad verbally and then followed it up with the bat. The result: Stuart Broad was taken off the attack two overs later. Even after his retirement, Sourav showed his aggression against Shane Warne during the first IPL encounter between Rajasthan Royals and Kolkata Knight Riders. Clearly, the Bengal tiger might have got old by then but his appetite for winning was clearly reflective by his actions on the field.

Sourav was equally aggressive as a batsman in his playing days and was dubbed as the 'God of Offside' by Rahul Dravid. His record in ODI speaks for himself with over 11,000 runs and 22 centuries. His record could have easily been better had he not relinquished the opener's slot to Virender Sehwag in ODIs. To add to his credentials, Sourav scored these runs at an average of 41.02 which is only bettered by the likes of Sachin Tendulkar (44.83), Jaques Kallis (44.36), Ricky Ponting (42.03) and Kumar Sangakkara (41.98). However, it is equally noteworthy to remember that his average in Tests also never went below 40 over 113 Test matches. The amount of runs that Sourav managed to score despite slump in his form during his captaincy and the period for which he was kept out of the team stand testimony to his ability to score runs at a fast pace.

Learning Tip

Aggression should always be matched with performance if it has to be made sustainable.

Sourav's aggression was also a result of his self-belief and his experience early on in his career. Sourav was dropped quite unceremoniously after just one ODI in 1992 and had to wait for four years before staging a comeback to the national team. It was this aggression that also fuelled his self-belief when he made his comeback to the Indian team amidst the adversity that existed. Sourav's upbringing in a wealthy family also contributed to his aggression as he normally got his way around. For someone who has always had to prove himself at every point in his cricketing life, aggression was ingrained in him. He was aggressive enough to have his way with the selectors in ensuring that a team is selected on merit regardless of the strength of the Mumbai, Delhi and South lobby that existed in Indian cricket. As captain, he ensured that youngsters were given fair amount of opportunities and no one is dropped after just one outing.

Consider for instance the case of Mahendra Singh Dhoni: In his first four matches for the country he had scored 0,12, 7* and 3. Yet, Sourav saw in him the aggressive wicketkeeper and believed that the player had a lot to contribute to the team. Dhoni reposed the faith in the captain by scoring 148 in the very next innings. There were talks about Yuvraj being dropped from the team as he too was considered as an inconsistent performer. Yet again, Sourav kept fighting for the young players and ensured that no one is dropped from the team and the team is selected on merit. Do you think that Team India was possible without having an aggressive leader like him at the helm of affairs? The concept that the Indian team can have small-town boys started during the era of Sourav. He used his aggression to groom a bunch of youngsters into a world beating team.

Imagine yourself in an office where your boss shows positive aggression and pushes you to achieve the goal as he or she believes in your abilities. If you perform poorly, he is the first one to scold you whereas if you succeed, he is equally lavish in his praise for your work. Such an attitude and coordinated aggression from the superiors brings about a positive atmosphere in the team. People start believing in their abilities and start focussing on the results rather than their place in the team.

Learning Tip

Controlled and well-directed aggression can
play a significant role in team building activities.

Sourav's aggression has not been limited to his cricketing days. Post his retirement, he has been part of the Cricket Advisory Committee (CAC) which was responsible for selection of the coach of Team India. Sourav yet again was quite vocal in his support for Anil Kumble during the selection process as well as during the fallout between Anil Kumble and Virat Kohli.

Even when Kumble relinquished the position of the coach, Sourav was equally vocal about the incident suggesting that it was his personal decision to do the same. Sourav has been equivocal in his support on the issue of revised pay structure for players in the domestic season and has brought up the issue in front of the technical committee of BCCI. Clearly, though Sourav has retired, he has not given up on his aggressive attitude. Unlike his professional life, Sourav is entirely different when it comes to his family and friends. It is almost like he has a switch to turn on or off his aggression levels. In a similar manner, as professionals, we must learn to control our stress levels at work and not be bogged down by it.

Learning Tip

Being aggressive is important part of your persona, but you must equally know how to control and channelize the same towards a goal.

There have been many cricketers before and after Sourav to have played for the country, yet Sourav stands out among them. He was arguably one of the finest left-handed batsman and a leader par excellence who created the transformation of Team India. There will be very few individuals who will have the same mental toughness and determination that defines him, builds his iconic status and makes him special for all of us. It would have perhaps been in the best interest of the game had Sourav not lost those precious years of his career due to various non-cricketing reasons. Indian cricket and its fans would have certainly been richer.

Extra Special Sourav

A. List of Sourav's Centuries

1. Test Centuries

No.	Score	Against	Pos.	Inn.	Venue	H/A	Date	Result
1	131	England	3	2	Lord's Cricket Ground, London	Away	20 Jun 96	Drawn
2	136	England	3	1	Trent Bridge, Nottingham	Away	04 Jul 96	Drawn
3	147	Sri Lanka	6	2	Sinhalese Sports Club, Colombo	Away	09 Aug 97	Drawn
4	109	Sri Lanka	6	2	Punjab Cricket Association Stadium, Mohali	Home	19 Nov 97	Drawn
5	173	Sri Lanka	4	1	Wankhede Stadium, Mumbai	Home	03 Dec 97	Drawn
6	101*	New Zealand	4	4	Seddon Park, Hamilton	Away	02 Jan 99	Drawn

No.	Score	Against	Pos.	Inn.	Venue	H/A	Date	Result
7	125	New Zealand	5	1	Sardar Patel Stadium, Ahmedabad	Home	29 Oct 99	Drawn
8	136	Zimbabwe	3	2	Feroz Shah Kotla, New Delhi	Home	28 Feb 02	Won
9	128	England	5	1	Headingley, Leeds	Away	22 Aug 02	Won
10	100*	New Zealand	6	1	Sardar Patel Stadium, Ahmedabad	Home	08 Oct 03	Drawn
11	144	Australia	5	2	Brisbane Cricket Ground, Brisbane	Away	04 Dec 03	Drawn
12	101	Zimbabwe	5	2	Queens Sports Club, Bulawayo	Away	13 Sep 05	Won
13	100	Bangladesh	5	1	Bir Shrestha Shahid Ruhul Amin Stadium, Chittagong	Away	18 May 07	Drawn
14	102	Pakistan	5	1	Eden Gardens, Kolkata	Home	30 Nov 07	Drawn
15	239	Pakistan	4	1	M. Chinnaswamy Stadium, Bangalore	Home	08 Dec 07	Drawn
16	102	Australia	6	1	Punjab Cricket Association Stadium, Mohali	Home	17 Oct 08	Won

Key: No.=Sl. No., Score=Score, Against=Team, Pos.=Batting position, Inn.=Innings number, S/R=Strike Rate, H/A/N=Home/Away/Neutral, Result=Match outcome

2. One-Day Centuries

No.	Score	Against	Pos.	Inn.	S/R	Venue	H/A/N	Result
1	113	Sri Lanka	2	1	89.68	R. Premadasa Stadium, Colombo	Away	Lost
2	124	Pakistan	1	2	89.85	Bangabandhu Stadium, Dhaka	Neutral	Won
3	105	New Zealand	2	1	75	Sharjah Cricket Association Stadium, Sharjah	Neutral	Won
4	109	Sri Lanka	1	1	80.14	R. Premadasa Stadium, Colombo	Away	Won
5	107*	Zimbabwe	2	2	82.94	Queens Sports Club, Bulawayo	Away	Won
6	130*	Sri Lanka	1	1	81.25	Vidarbha Cricket Association Ground, Nagpur	Home	Won
7	183	Sri Lanka	2	1	115.82	County Ground, Taunton	Neutral	Won
8	139	Zimbabwe	2	1	94.55	Gymkhana Club Ground, Nairobi	Neutral	Won
9	153*	New Zealand	1	1	102	Captain Roop Singh Stadium, Gwalior	Home	Won
10	100	Australia	2	2	78.74	Melbourne Cricket Ground, Melbourne	Away	Lost
11	141	Pakistan	2	1	97.91	Adelaide Oval, Adelaide	Neutral	Won
12	105*	South Africa	1	2	75.53	Keenan Stadium, Jamshedpur	Home	Won
13	135*	Bangladesh	1	2	108.87	Bangabandhu Stadium, Dhaka	Away	Won
14	141*	South Africa	1	1	99.29	Gymkhana Club Ground, Nairobi	Neutral	Won

No.	Score	Against	Pos.	Inn.	S/R	Venue	H/A/N	Result
15	117	New Zealand	1	1	90	Gymkhana Club Ground, Nairobi	Neutral	Lost
16	144	Zimbabwe	2	1	94.73	Sardar Patel Stadium, Ahmedabad	Home	Won
17	127	South Africa	1	1	100.79	New Wanderers Stadium, Johannesburg	Away	Lost
18	111	Kenya	1	1	89.51	Boland Park, Paarl	Neutral	Won
19	117*	England	2	2	107.33	R. Premadasa Stadium, Colombo	Neutral	Won
20	112*	Namibia	3	1	94.11	City Oval, Pietermaritzburg	Neutral	Won
21	107*	Kenya	3	2	89.16	Newlands Cricket Ground, Cape Town	Neutral	Won
22	111*	Kenya	3	1	97.36	Sahara Stadium Kingsmead, Durban	Neutral	Won

Key: No.=Sl. No., Score=Score, Against=Team, Pos.=Batting position, Inn.=Innings number, S/R=Strike Rate, H/A/N=Home/Away/Neutral, Result=Match outcome

B. List of the Man of the Match Awards

1. ODIs

Date	Vs	Ground	Bat	Bowl	Ca
04-02-1997	South Africa	Buffalo Park	83		0
24-07-1997	Bangladesh	Sinhalese Sports Club Ground	73*	0/24	1
14-09-1997	Pakistan	Cricket, Skating & Curling Club	32	2/16	1

Date	Vs	Ground	Bat	Bowl	Ca
18-09-1997	Pakistan	Cricket, Skating & Curling Club	2	5/16	1
20-09-1997	Pakistan	Cricket, Skating & Curling Club	75*	2/29	0
21-09-1997	Pakistan	Cricket, Skating & Curling Club	96	2/33	0
30-09-1997	Pakistan	National Stadium	89	0/39	0
18-01-1998	Pakistan	Bangabandhu National Stadium	124	0/5	0
19-06-1998	Sri Lanka	R Premadasa Stadium	80		0
12-09-1998	Pakistan	Cricket, Skating & Curling Club	54*	3/33	0
27-09-1998	Zimbabwe	Queens Sports Club	107*		1
22-03-1999	Sri Lanka	Vidarbha Cricket Association Ground	130*	4/21	0
04-04-1999	Pakistan	M Chinnaswamy Stadium	13	2/35	0
26-05-1999	Sri Lanka	County Ground (Taunton)	183	0/37	0
29-05-1999	England	Edgbaston	40	3/27	0
11-09-1999	West Indies	Cricket, Skating & Curling Club	54*		0
01-10-1999	Zimbabwe	Gymkhana Club Ground	139		0
11-11-1999	New Zealand	Captain Roop Singh Stadium	153*	1/33	0
17-11-1999	New Zealand	Feroz Shah Kotla	86	1/29	0
25-01-2000	Pakistan	Adelaide Oval	141		0
12-03-2000	South Africa	Keenan Stadium	105*		1
30-05-2000	Bangladesh	Bangabandhu National Stadium	135*	0/35	0
13-10-2000	South Africa	Gymkhana Club Ground	141*	1/5	1
05-12-2000	Zimbabwe	Sardar Patel Stadium	144		0

Date	Vs	Ground	Bat	Bowl	Ca
11-12-2000	Zimbabwe	Green Park	71*	5/34	0
19-10-2001	South Africa	Buffalo Park	85		1
10-03-2002	Zimbabwe	Punjab Cricket Association is Bindra Stadium	86		0
07-03-2003	Kenya	Newlands	107*		0
20-03-2003	Kenya	Kingsmead	111*		0
05-09-2004	England	Lord's	90		0
11-09-2004	Kenya	The Rose Bowl	90	0/21	2
02-09-2007	England	Headingley	59	2/26	0
No. of Man of the Match awards = 32					

Key: Date=date of match, Vs=Versus, Ground=Venue, Inns=Innings, Bat=Batting Score, Bowl=Bowling figure, Ca=Catches

2. Tests

Date	Vs	Ground	Inns	Bat	Bowl	Ca
04-07-1996	England	Trent Bridge	1st	136	3/71	0
			2nd	48		0
03-12-1997	Sri Lanka	Wankhede Stadium	1st	173	0/19	0
			2nd	11		0
22-08-2001	Sri Lanka	Asgiriya Stadium	1st	18	2/69	0
			2nd	98*	0/21	0
04-12-2003	Australia	Brisbane Cricket Ground	1st	144	0/8	0
			2nd	DNB		0
08-12-2007	Pakistan	M Chinnaswamy Stadium	1st	239	1/20	0
			2nd	91		0
11-04-2008	South Africa	Green Park	1st	87		1
			2nd	13*		1

Date	Vs	Ground	Inns	Bat	Bowl	Ca
No. of Man of the Match awards = 6						

Key: Date=date of match, Vs=Versus, Ground=Venue, Inns=Innings, Bat=Batting Score, Bowl=Bowling figure, Ca=Catches

C. Comparison with other Captains

Table 1
Success Rate of Various Captains in ODI Cricket

Player	Span	Mat	Won	Lost	Tied	NR	%W
R.T. Ponting (AUS/ICC)	2002–2012	230	165	51	2	12	76.14
W.J. Cronje (SA)	1994–2000	138	99	35	1	3	73.7
S.R. Waugh (AUS)	1997–2002	106	67	35	3	1	65.23
I.V.A. Richards (WI)	1980–1991	105	67	36	0	2	65.04
G.C. Smith (Afr/SA)	2003–2011	150	92	51	1	6	64.23
Wasim Akram (PAK)	1993–2000	109	66	41	2	0	61.46
A.R. Border (AUS)	1985–1994	178	107	67	1	3	61.42
A.B. de Villiers (SA)	2012–2017	103	59	39	1	4	60.1
M.S. Dhoni (INDIA)	2007–2016	199	110	74	4	11	59.57
D.P.M.D. Jayawardene (Asia/SL)	2004–2013	129	71	49	1	8	59.09
S.T. Jayasuriya (SL)	1998–2003	118	66	47	2	3	58.26
Imran Khan (PAK)	1982–1992	139	75	59	1	4	55.92
M. Azharuddin (INDIA)	1990–1999	174	90	76	2	6	54.16
S.C. Ganguly (Asia/INDIA)	1999–2005	147	76	66	0	5	53.52
B.C. Lara (WI)	1994–2007	125	59	59	0	7	50
A. Ranatunga (SL)	1988–1999	193	89	95	1	8	48.37
S.P. Fleming (NZ)	1997–2007	218	98	106	1	13	48.04

Key: Mat=Matches, Won=Matches won, Lost=Matches lost, Tied=Matches tied, NR=No Result, %W=Win percentage

Table 2
Success Rate of Various Captains in Test Cricket as of 10 February 2018

Player	Span	Mat	Won	Lost	Tied	Draw	W/L	%W	%L
S.R. Waugh (AUS)	1999–2004	57	41	9	0	7	4.55	71.92	15.78
R.T. Ponting (AUS)	2004–10	77	48	16	0	13	3	62.33	20.77
I.V.A. Richards (WI)	1980–91	50	27	8	0	15	3.37	54	16
M.A. Taylor (AUS)	1994–99	50	26	13	0	11	2	52	26
M.J. Clarke (AUS)	2011–15	47	24	16	0	7	1.5	51.06	34.04
M.P. Vaughan (ENG)	2003–08	51	26	11	0	14	2.36	50.98	21.56
W.J. Cronje (SA)	1994–2000	53	27	11	0	15	2.45	50.94	20.75
P.B.H. May (ENG)	1955–61	41	20	10	0	11	2	48.78	24.39
C.H. Lloyd (WI)	1974–85	74	36	12	0	26	3	48.64	16.21
G.C. Smith (ICC/SA)	2003–14	109	53	29	0	27	1.82	48.62	26.6
A.J. Strauss (ENG)	2006–12	50	24	11	0	15	2.18	48	22
Misbah-ul-Haq (PAK)	2010–17	56	26	19	0	11	1.36	46.42	33.92
M.S. Dhoni (INDIA)	2008–14	60	27	18	0	15	1.5	45	30
G.S. Chappell (AUS)	1975–83	48	21	13	0	14	1.61	43.75	27.08
S.C. Ganguly (INDIA)	2000–05	49	21	13	0	15	1.61	42.85	26.53
A.N. Cook (ENG)	2010–16	59	24	22	0	13	1.09	40.67	37.28
N. Hussain (ENG)	1999-2003	45	17	15	0	13	1.13	37.77	33.33
S.P. Fleming (NZ)	1997-2006	80	28	27	0	25	1.03	35	33.75
A.R. Border (AUS)	1984–94	93	32	22	1	38	1.45	34.4	23.65
M. Azharuddin (INDIA)	1990–99	47	14	14	0	19	1	29.78	29.78

Imran Khan (PAK)	1982–92	48	14	8	0	26	1.75	29.16	16.66
MA Atherton (ENG)	1993-2001	54	13	21	0	20	0.61	24.07	38.88
Nawab of Pataudi (INDIA)	1962–75	40	9	19	0	12	0.47	22.5	47.5
A. Ranatunga (SL)	1989–99	56	12	19	0	25	0.63	21.42	33.92
B.C. Lara (WI)	1997-2006	47	10	26	0	11	0.38	21.27	55.31
S.M. Gavaskar (INDIA)	1976–85	47	9	8	0	30	1.12	19.14	17.02

Key: Mat=Matches, Won=Matches won, Lost=Matches lost, Tied=Matches tied, Draw=Matches drawn, W/L=Matches won/Matches lost, NR=No Result, %W=Win percentage, %L=Loss percentage

D. Records and Achievements

- The only cricketer to win four consecutive man of the match awards in One Day Internationals.
- The eighth highest run-scorer in ODI history and second among the Indians, with 11,363 runs.
- The second fastest batsman to reach 9,000 ODI runs after AB De Villiers of South Africa who broke Ganguly's record in 2017.
- One of the only five cricketers to have achieved the unique treble of 10,000 runs, 100 wickets & 100 catches in ODI cricket.
- Has the highest individual score by an Indian batsman (183) in the Cricket World Cup.
- One of the 14 cricketers in the world to have played 100 or more Tests and 300 or more ODIs.
- India's most successful Test captain overseas, winning 11 out of 28 matches that he led.

- Holds the record in ODIs for highest runs as opening partnership along with Sachin Tendulkar for 8,227 runs.

E. List of Awards

- Arjuna Award, 1998
- Ceat Cricketer of the Year, 1999–2000
- Ceat Indian Captain of the Year, 2001–2002
- Wisden 6th Best All-time ODI Batsman, 2002
- Award for Cricketing Excellence, 2003
- Padma Shri, 2004 (4th highest civilian award in India)
- Banga Bibhushan Award, 2013

Acknowledgements

This book would not have been possible without the blessings of my late mother (Dr Lina Bhattacharya). She had been instrumental in guiding me and whatever I have achieved in life is owed to her. I would like to thank my father (Vishwa Nath Bhattacharya) and my elder brother Abhishek and sister-in-law Pamela who have constantly supported me through every phase in my life.

I would like to express my gratitude for my publisher Rupa Publications, the editorial team (Elina Majumdar and Anurupa Sen) and my commissioning editor Shambhu Sahu for giving me the opportunity to write this book. I would also like to express my gratitude towards my friends Prashant, Biswarup, Sujit, Sushil, Ashima, Vikram, Kushan and Anuradha for putting their faith in my abilities at all times in my life.